ALASKA NATIONAL PARKLANDS

THIS LAST TREASURE

William E. Brown, *writer*

Carolyn Elder, *compiler*

Christina Watkins, *designer*

Catherine Rezabeck, *coordinator*

Published by the
Alaska Natural History Association
Anchorage, Alaska 99501

This book is dedicated to Margaret E. Murie — pioneer Alaskan, conservationist, writer, and inspirational realist in the modern world.

Newton Drury, when he was Director of the National Park Service, said: "Surely the great United States of America is not so poor we cannot afford to have these places, nor so rich that we can do without them."

When all the nonrenewable resources have been dug up, hauled away, piped away, to satisfy the needs of a certain span of users, Alaska can still have a renewable, self-perpetuating resource of inestimable value — value economical, value spiritual, value for the health of the people.

We cannot foretell the future, but we can give a nod toward it by putting this last treasure of wild country into an interest-bearing savings account.

In the long view — all Alaska needs to do is be Alaska.

Margaret Murie, testifying
in favor of the Alaska
Lands Act of 1980

FOREWORD

I write with two views of Alaska. Out one window, blue sky frames jagged peaks of the Chugach Mountains, mottled with snow and spring's encroaching green. Turning, I watch a raven glide over spruce and birch, coasting on a downdraft toward Cook Inlet's glacial tidewaters. Distantly, where the Chigmit Mountains hinge the Alaska and Aleutian Ranges, snowfields and clouds blur in a sun-shot sky misty with ocean moisture.

These convenient scenes — moving with the wind, changing with the season — tie me to the larger Alaska beyond the two visible horizons. Past those sharp peaks lies interior Alaska of boundless forest, broad river valley, rimming mountain range. Still farther, arctic desert meets ice-locked sea under dry polar air. The other misty distance marks the edge of the warm sea, whose winds and currents spawn the storms of maritime Alaska. Extending nearly 3,000 miles, this wave-lashed coast of glacial fjords and volcanic isles skirts the North Pacific from rain forest to barren Aleutian outpost.

Scale and diversity foil all who try to simplify Alaska. Its immense and ceaseless grandeur numbs the mind, glazes the eye, and plagues the writer who would describe it. The intellect cannot close the suitcase on this subcontinent. Always a spare peninsula or archipelago or coastal plain dangles out after the sweaty struggle to buckle the straps.

So this book about Alaska's national parklands is not a synthesis. It is instead episodic and impressionistic.

It lends human scale to vast landscapes and cosmic events by borrowing the perceptions of explorers, scientists, and artists — both visitors and native to the land. The choice of words and pictures is intuitive. They all support the idea that Alaska is a gathering of mythic landscapes, asked to meet here by God or Nature.

This book does not record the recent history of travail and antagonism that established the newer parklands — the poles of philosophy finally compromised in the Alaska Lands Act of 1980. It simply accepts with gratitude the triumph of enduring values, which spring from these places and gain strength in their preservation.

WEB

A few years ago a man from a New York foundation took a night flight in a small plane from Nome to King Salmon, a straight-line distance of 500 miles across western Alaska. This usually talkative man said hardly a word during the three-hour flight. Fellow travelers noted that he stayed glued to the window, peering into the cloudless darkness below. When he got off the plane he said only, "I didn't see a single light." Then he went to his room.

Another traveler took a trip in a skin boat with an Eskimo elder. The land was featureless to the traveler's eyes. Periodically the old Eskimo pulled ashore.

"We get fresh water in a pond behind that bank."

"Berries are ripe along this stream."

"Walk quietly to that hill, you will see caribou."

"We will catch fish here, and camp there, out of the wind."

Everything was as he said.

Alaska is a wilderness to some. To others it is a homeland, completely mapped in the mind.

CONTENTS

INTRODUCTION

Long-time Alaska resident Ginny Hill Wood believes that Alaska's most valuable resource is space, ". . . spectacularly beautiful space that is not all filled up with people and industry as is so much of the rest of the world." These spaces bring home to us the fact that no matter how much we alter the surface of the world to insulate ourselves from natural forces, they are in control. We are parts of the biological system they created, totally dependent on them.

It is comforting to know that in large parts of Alaska, Nature is alive and well. In these remote places, observing Nature at her timeless tasks, we sense the spiritual qualities of wilderness. In all eras, particularly troubled ones, people have sought the wild places. In communion with what is timeless, we gain perspective on what is temporal and can put aside the false and fleeting.

The national parklands in Alaska, some 50 million acres of them, hold in trust the closest approximations to complete ecosystems left on this planet. Their value — as links in a cosmic process that began long before we came and will continue long after we go — is beyond utilitarian concern. Yet, they are useful in human terms, as citadels of cultural ideals and as fields of special endeavor and understanding.

These parklands embrace terrestrial and marine geographies representative of all major environments of Alaska. In latitude they range from temperate southeast Alaska to the Arctic. Longitudinally, they span the state — from Yukon headwaters to Bering Strait and the looming shores of Siberia.

No one can see this immense territory in a hurry. Climates and weather conditions vary incredibly, even in summer. Selection of clothing and gear confounds the most experienced trekker. Logistics are tenuous. It is well, then, to select objectives carefully, to equip for all conditions, and to build slippage into travel schedules.

Alaska parklands can be ranked into three kinds of spaces:

1. Those that meet visitor expectations for traditional national park access, staffing, and facilities.

2. Intermediate spaces where access and visitor aids are rudimentary — equivalent to undeveloped or wilderness parklands in other states.

3. Outback spaces where visitors will be entirely on their own — wilderness in an absolute sense, compounded by size, weather, and terrain factors only rarely approximated elsewhere.

Only the developed sectors and access zones of the older Alaska parks meet the traditional criteria. The intermediate group includes some sectors of the new parklands, especially those connecting with Alaska's limited road system. All the rest, at least 95 percent of the Alaska parks, monuments, and preserves, fit the outback description. The remote sectors of the old parks may be the wildest places of all since no sport or subsistence hunting is allowed there. (The Alaska Lands Act of 1980 protects subsistence hunting in most of the new park and monument lands and allows both sport and subsistence hunting in the preserves.)

Visitors, whether traveling independently or with a group, can match their capabilities with the different environments — ranging from traditional parklands to primitive or hazard areas. People can sample many combinations, both within individual parklands and amongst them. The wealth of landscape mosaics invites every kind of experience from fully directed tour, through intermediate or near-wild adventure, to remote trek, climb, or river float.

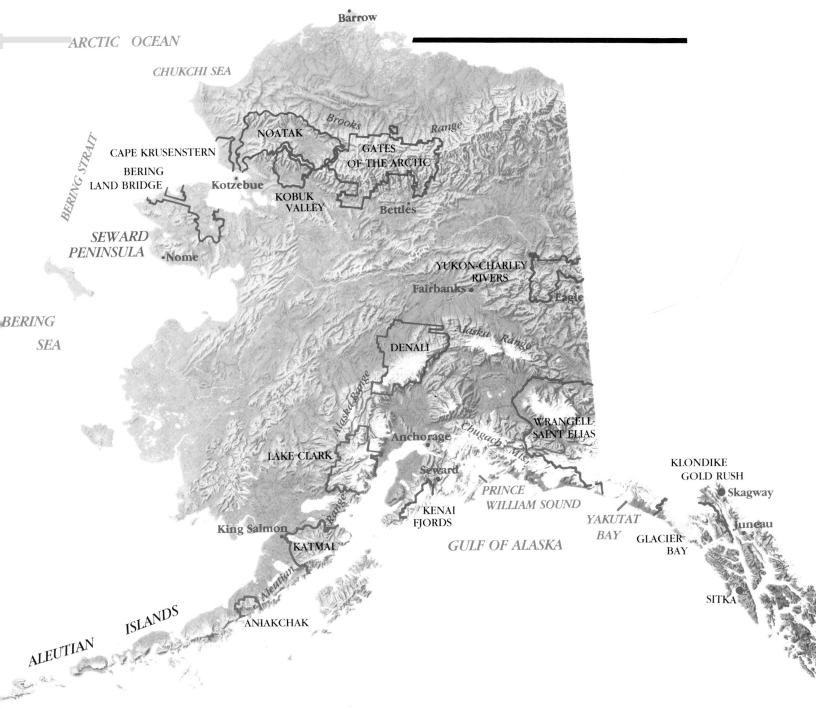

ARCTIC OCEAN

CHUKCHI SEA

Barrow

BERING STRAIT

Brooks   Range

NOATAK

CAPE KRUSENSTERN

BERING
LAND BRIDGE

Kotzebue

GATES
OF THE ARCTIC

KOBUK
VALLEY

Bettles

SEWARD
PENINSULA

Nome

BERING

SEA

YUKON-CHARLEY
RIVERS

Fairbanks

Eagle

Alaska   Range

DENALI

Alaska Range

WRANGELL-
SAINT ELIAS

Chugach Mts.

LAKE CLARK

Anchorage

KLONDIKE
GOLD RUSH

Seward

PRINCE
WILLIAM SOUND

Skagway

Range

KENAI
FJORDS

YAKUTAT
BAY

GLACIER
BAY

Juneau

King Salmon

GULF OF ALASKA

KATMAI

Aleutian

ALEUTIAN   ISLANDS

ANIAKCHAK

SITKA

These have been the basics of preparation. More important for fulfillment and warm welcome is the philosophy of approach.

Anthropologist Colin Turnbull has commented on the often frustrated pilgrimage of people to far places. Though he writes of tourists to East Africa, disappointed by their insulated and artificial experiences there, his observations have universal application. He reflects on the causes of frustration:

> "We thought it would be more primitive" is a frequently heard comment. It is an innocent observation, devoid of insult; for many, *primitive* conveys not so much backwardness as some kind of primal truth, referring to a state when man and nature lived in harmony, rather than locked in combat.
>
> The average tourists — confined to the safari circuit and organized groups — are carefully kept at a distance from all that they observe: the animals, the land, the people. They are denied the opportunity many of them sought: to make contact with something of their not-so-remote past. . . .
> They are denied the opportunity to escape from a world of artifice and manipulation.[1]

Turnbull then describes the kinds of contact that eluded these people, leaving them unfulfilled. Times to be alone, to touch, to listen. Times to sense the powers in sacred places and the mystic connections between animals and humans living as integral parts of the natural world.

Because the Alaska national parklands are so predominantly wild, even on the thresholds of the few developed sites, the escape from artifice is easy. It does not take the full-scale wilderness plunge to find places where the land sets its terms and people conform to them.

Sensitivity to Alaska's cultural environments opens the possibility of rewarding human contact. With patience, visitors may gain insight into lifeways that let them see, in Turnbull's phrase, their "lost identity" as hunters and gatherers. Both Native and non-Native Alaskans perpetuate traditions that spring from ancient cultures or more recent frontier experience. Many of these people subsist within the newer parklands as cultural components of the ecosystem.

The basic courtesies of any human contact should be observed scrupulously in subsistence camps. Cultural privacy is prized in bush communities. Disturbance of cabins, equipment, or fishnets is a serious form of trespass. Becoming a burden to people fully occupied with hunting and fishing deprives them of their sustenance.

Even so, there is usually opportunity for friendship and the sharing of coffee around a campfire. Such moments, as darkness gathers and the river flows by, bring flickering memories of other campfires and other times in a history shared by all.

The Alaska National Interest Lands Conservation Act of 1980 placed large parts of Alaska in the nation's conservation, wilderness, and recreation systems — wild and scenic rivers, forests, wildlife refuges, and parks. Combined with the older federal reserves and a growing state park system, these new designations round out a protected land base unsurpassed anywhere.

The National Park System in Alaska comprises 15 administrative units, which together cover a wide spectrum of scenic, scientific, cultural, and recreational values. Each reflects a different facet of gleaming Alaska. Each perpetuates a vital part of the Great Land, adding outstanding natural and cultural treasures to America's protected heritage. All of them are treated in the pages that follow.

The order of presentation takes its cue from the concentrics of Alaska's geography — the lines of geologic history traced by the Pacific shore and the great mountain ranges that traverse the state. Thus: the Pacific Rim, the Interior, and the Far North parklands.

ALASKA NATIONAL PARKLANDS

THE PACIFIC RIM

Alaska's Pacific Rim is a zone of tension, a meeting place of fundamental natural forces. Structurally, segments of Earth's granitic crust converge like pieces of a gigantic jig-saw puzzle. One segment, the Pacific Plate, plunges under the North American Plate and lifts it, thereby powering the mountain building, earthquakes, and volcanism that shape and shake this landscape. Here too, warm and cold seas meet with one another; and, moved by tide and current, they sweep into bays and fjords and swirl about multitudes of islands. Even the atmosphere seems in conflict with itself. Arctic and Pacific air masses whirl about the Aleutian storm center, then assault the bordering shores with wind and wave, rain and snow. On this frontier between warm and cold latitudes the descending moisture is slowed in its return to the sea. Deep snows become perennial. They compact into icefields and glaciers that sculpt the mountains and in places flow grandly to tidewater.

The dynamics and extremes of the physical world are matched by a rich and diverse biota. Here mingle plants and animals of temperate, subarctic, and arctic types in a profusion of marine, intertidal, and terrestrial environments. Plant communities range from towering rain forests to pioneering colonies of lichen and moss huddled on frigid rock. In the zones where warm and cold waters meet, billions of tiny organisms enrich the food chain that feeds other hosts of fish and marine mammals. Along streams turned red by spawning salmon, bears and eagles congregate. And at the turn of seasons, migrant birds from many continents arrive or depart these shores.

Humans long ago discovered these resources. They dwelt in the margins between mountain and sea — Indian, Aleut, Eskimo. Compared to other parts of Alaska these Pacific rimlands were bountiful. Fish and marine mammals — predictable and in great numbers — supported large populations of people oriented to the sea and the spawning streams. Complex societies sprang from differing cultural roots that were attuned to specific environments. Yet there were many cultural similarities based on the common quest for marine products and migrating salmon.

Europeans eventually came to these same shores, first as explorers and fur traders. Their clashes with the aboriginal people and with each other seemed to mirror the natural tensions at work in the rimland. The Russians came first, pressing Aleuts into service as sea otter hunters. The pelts brought huge profits in the China market, which soon attracted explorers and traders from other nations.

For a century after the Russians began their incursions in the 1740s, European interest in Alaska remained fixed on the Pacific coastal region. Only gradually did explorers, fur traders, whalers, and miners penetrate the remoter parts of Alaska. To this day the Pacific Rim contains the greater part of Alaska's population — testimony to its ease of access, comparatively mild climate, and natural riches.

Starting with Ice Age hunters who pursued mammals across the Bering Land Bridge from Siberia, Alaska has attracted waves of adventurers and exploiters. They sought furs, whales, gold, fish, timber, and, lately, oil. But throughout its history, as evidenced by oral tradition and written record, there have been other Sirens that enticed people to this remote and often inhospitable place. The challenge of the unknown called explorers and cartographers, many of whom disappeared in the blank spaces on their charts. Scientists, too, found irresistable Alaska's primordial wilds, its strangely adapted life forms, its exotic societies.

Many who came here, for whatever practical or visionary purpose, wrote of their experiences. Memoirs and reports carried their words and pictures to a world

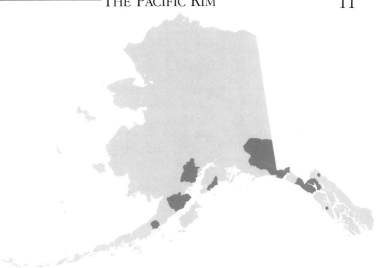

becoming ever more domesticated. Thus did Alaska become a place of pilgrimage, a wondrous place to see before one died. Here was one last place on earth where people could still experience what Sigurd F. Olson has called the Primal Heritage, ". . . values born of timelessness, mystery, the great silences, and an ancient way of life."

The first part of the present pilgrimage begins in

Alaska's Southeast Panhandle, then sweeps around the Pacific Rim to the Alaska Peninsula. Within this 900-mile arc are eight parklands representative of the natural and cultural themes just sketched.

*Impending
cataclysms are
in its look . . .*

In settings of wild beauty, Glacier Bay unites the powers of mountains, ice, and the sea. Its high places, pure and serene, overlook far-reaching arms and inlets of the sea. Shorelines of the bay trace contours of glacial excavation. The passage from the forested lower bay to the bedrock and ice-bound upper bay skirts islands scored by glaciers. It enters inlets deep and narrow, headed by cascading glaciers, and others shallow and broad, filled with the silt of glacial rivers. The Fairweather Range separates the bay from the Outer Coast, a wild, abandoned place lashed by storms off the Gulf of Alaska. And constantly, all around the headlands and swirling in the coves, currents and tides are at work. Amidst scenes of devastation and turbulence, living things in great numbers find sustenance — their environment determined by the long cycles of glacial advance and retreat. Glacier Bay's stark contrasts expose the primal forces that shape the earth and populate it with life.

The processes that stir this landscape have inspired a great cultural adventure — expressed through art, philosophy, and scientific study. Nature's explicit flow compelled these expressions. For here is a place where geologic history moves at a pace measurable during a human lifetime, where biological succession produces radical change in a decade. It is scenery set in motion by the destructive and regenerative forces that contend here.

When English navigator George Vancouver sailed these waters less than two centuries ago, he described and charted Glacier Bay as a recess in the shoreline only a few miles deep, "terminated by compact solid mountains of ice rising perpendicularly from the water's edge." The Glacier Bay of today, a deepwater fjord system 65 miles long, was filled by a gigantic glacier fed by ice fields in the "lofty frozen mountains" bounding it. Since then, rapid retreat of this master glacier has opened the mountain fastness to the probing sea.

In Vancouver's time, Bartlett Cove in the lower bay was covered by the glacier. Today the cove's bordering mainland and islands support a Sitkan rain forest — huge trees where only a moment ago in geologic time was ice, then bare rock, then the beginnings of plant life and soil formation. This is the miracle that has fascinated scientists. In this intertwined history of ice and plants is the record of glacial advance and recession, of life being overwhelmed by surging glaciers, then quickly reestablishing itself in the wake of retreating ice.

On the shores of Glacier Bay in 1890, John Muir noted the beginnings of a new forest and the remains of an ancient one that had flourished before the last glacial advance. Later, William S. Cooper carried forth the studies of plant succession and relic forests that would reveal the bay's botanical and glacial history. Through the Ecological Society of America, he urged protection of the bay's unique values as a natural laboratory. Based on these efforts, President Coolidge in 1925 established Glacier Bay National Monument.

A trip up bay traverses the recent history of glacial retreat. From Bartlett Cove to the face of the glaciers the plants decline in size as on a graph. Reversing the order of plant succession, the big trees fade out and shrubs take over. Finally, the level of life descends to dwarf-plant pioneers scattered in glacial debris. The colors of life pale as rock and ice replace the dwindling vegetation. In the extreme reaches of the fjords, earth's structure stands naked — the world before life, the building blocks of the first days.

Geographically and ecologically this landscape is separated into isolated parts or "islands." Mountains and arms of the sea channel plant and animal life just as they channel the flow of glaciers. Animals follow the pioneering plants as they revegetate those places just freed from ice. The mobility of large mammals — moose, bears, goats, wolves — allows them to cross ice barrens and mountains or swim narrow waters in their search for living space. But small mammals, blocked by such barriers, may be isolated in this constantly

changing terrain.

Seasonally, the tide-flushed waters of Glacier Bay surge with life. Exploding populations of shrimplike krill and tiny fish attract seals, whales, and great rafts of birds. Glacier Bay is summer home for humpback whales. These magnificent creatures and people — the one species endangered, the other possibly endangering — uneasily share the bay's narrow waters as scientists observe and ponder.

First sightings by Europeans of the Glacier Bay region were from the open sea. At great distances they saw the stunning line of the Saint Elias Mountains and the Fairweather Range. As they sailed nearer, Mount Fairweather reared up nearly 3 miles above sea level, dominating the entire Outer Coast. Both Native and European voyagers feared the violence of this wave-battered shore nearly devoid of sheltered waters. True, the beachline breaks at Lituya Bay; but rip tides and topping seas guard its entrance. Heading on a geologic fault, it is a place of earthquakes and giant waves. Human tragedies mark its history.

At the far northwest corner of the parkland, the Alsek River cuts a low-altitude valley from interior Canada to the sea. A major river, burdened by glacial debris, it maintains its course by eroding the rising mountains through which it flows. This natural corridor has allowed animals and people to migrate through the mountain chains that otherwise isolate the Outer Coast.

At Glacier Bay, natural powers converge to release great energies. The sense of these powers invokes mythic gods and apprehensions beyond all normal experience. For people ancient and modern this has been the central meaning of Glacier Bay. Beginning with the writings of John Muir, and for a generation thereafter, Glacier Bay became the archetype of Alaska. Its extraordinary reality exceeded all imaginings about Alaska. It introduced the rest of the world to this great land, all the while promising new wonders beyond its lofty frozen mountains. ■

After supper, crouching about a dull fire of fossil wood, . . . [my Indian guides] became still more doleful, and talked in tones that accorded well with the wind and waters and growling torrents about us, telling sad stories of crushed canoes, drowned Indians, and hunters frozen in snowstorms.

. . . the clouds began to rise from the lower altitudes, slowly lifting their white skirts, and lingering in majestic, wing-shaped masses about the mountains that rise out of the broad, icy sea. These were the highest and whitest of all the white mountains, and the greatest of all the glaciers I had yet seen. Climbing higher for a still broader outlook, I made notes and sketched, improving the precious time while sunshine streamed through the luminous fringes of the clouds, and fell on the green waters of the fjord, the glittering bergs, the crystal bluffs of the two vast glaciers, the intensely white, far-spreading fields of ice, and the ineffably chaste and spiritual heights of the Fairweather Range, which were now hidden, now partly revealed, the whole making a picture of icy wildness unspeakably pure and sublime.

John Muir, 1879[1]

Probably few more strange and impressive spectacles than this glacier affords can be found on the continent. It has a curious fascination. Impending cataclysms are in its look. In a moment or two you know some part of it will topple or slide into the sea.

We saw the world-shaping forces at work; we scrambled over plains they had built but yesterday. We saw them transport enormous rocks, and tons on tons of soil and debris from the distant mountains; we saw the remains of extensive forests they had engulfed probably within the century, and were now uncovering again; we saw their turbid rushing streams loaded with newly ground rocks and soil-making material; we saw the beginnings of vegetation in the tracks of the retreating glacier; our dredgers brought up the first forms of sea life along the shore; we witnessed the formation of the low mounds and ridges and bowl-shaped depressions that so often diversify our landscapes — all the while with the muffled thunder of the falling bergs in our ears.

... great blue bergs rise up from below — born of the depths. The enormous pressure to which their particles have been subjected for many centuries seems to have intensified their color. They have a pristine, elemental look. Their crystals have not seen the light since they fell in snowflakes back amid the mountains generations ago. All this time imprisoned, traveling in darkness, carving the valleys, polishing the rocks, under a weight as of mountains, till at last their deliverance comes with crash and roar and they are once more free to career in the air and light as dew or rain or cloud, and then again to be drawn into that cycle of transformation and caught and bound once more in glacier chains for another century.

John Burroughs, 1899[2]

But the sound lingers on when one has heard.
Down the centuries the booming primeval thunder.

Dave Bohn[3]

Most of the earth's glaciers have been shrinking in recent decades, but in no locality have observations revealed more spectacular recession than in the Muir Inlet arm of Glacier Bay in Southeastern Alaska. . . . Because of the rapidity of this recession and the comparatively long record of fairly detailed observations, this area provides a unique opportunity for studying the various phenomena associated with shrinking glaciers and the emergence from under the ice of new land and marine features. Here is offered an example on a small scale of conditions which have

prevailed many times in geologic history during the waning of the continental ice sheets and which in future may affect millions of square miles of the earth's surface now buried beneath glacial ice.

William O. Field, Jr.[4]

"Muir Glacier, Alaska" by Thomas Hill courtesy of the Anchorage Historical and Fine Arts Museum

A feature of unique interest in the Glacier Bay region is the presence of relics of an earlier forest which flourished prior to the last glacial advance.

At one locality in Muir Inlet, the relics were found to be remarkably well preserved. The trunks, numbering at least two hundred, stood thickly together. Many still retained their bark, with mosses clinging to it. Small trees and the lower branches of large ones were many of them intact to the smallest twig. The humus layer which covered the rock surfaces was mostly thin and hard, almost skin-like, but in places there were sheets of perfectly preserved forest mosses.

The presence of these relics provides clear proof that some centuries ago the ice fields surrounding Glacier Bay were more contracted than they are today. At that time the surrounding mountains were clothed with a forest which was identical in every way with the forest of similar habitat and stage of development in southeastern Alaska today. The peaceful order of its life was suddenly disturbed by the invasion of ice tongues which descended from the higher mountains, coalesced into broad piedmont expanses, and finally united to form one huge glacier. The forest upon the upper mountain sides was swept clean away, and that upon the lower slopes and the lowlands was buried beneath hundreds of feet of sediments deposited by glacial streams during the advance. Over all poured the great ice flood, thousands of feet deep.

About 200 years ago, the glaciers began to recede, revealing the ancient forests, and opening an ever-widening expanse of bare ground to renewed invasion by plants.

adapted from William S. Cooper[5]

Thus the cycles continue: a new forest is developing today amidst the remnants of the old. Radio-carbon dating, discovered since Cooper's time, proves that some of the trees stood alive more than 7,000 years ago. It is not inconceivable that evidence of man will be found among the relics, for Tlingit legend tells of ancestors driven out of their homeland by advancing ice.

We have concluded that there are many infallible signs of rain in this region. If the sun shines, if the stars appear, if there are clouds or if there are none; these are all sure indications. If the barometer falls it will rain; if the barometer rises, it will rain; if the barometer remains steady, it will continue to rain.

Harry Fielding Reid, 1892[6]

As I sit now and type I can still hear, in the inevitable rain on the roof, the distant roar of the Casement River; the sound of glacier-becoming-sea. And I can also hear the silence of snowflakes falling in the peaks of the high Fairweathers: the sea-becoming-glacier. All the processes which created Glacier Bay over the millennia are still at work today. The landscape is in constant flux, all the elements are in perpetual motion, everything seems to be on its way to becoming something else. The Fairweathers thrust ever higher into the sky and catch more snow which compresses to ice which flows back to the sea which runs back and forth in tides and constantly erodes the glaciers at one end while it constantly renews them at the other as it rises into the air on winds and falls as snow in the high peaks. Life accommodates itself to the vagaries of this crazy scheme, following the ice as it retreats, yielding powerlessly where the glaciers have begun a new comeback. . . .

Carolyn Elder

On my last evening in the Beardsley Islands I took a walk along the beach to see the sunset over the mountains. It was a beautiful evening — such as you rarely see nowadays in the South 48 — with utmost clarity in every direction. A coyote shared the beach with me, which they were wont to do, walking a ways ahead of me. I was also sharing the island with a black bear and her cub — so stayed well out in the open to give her fair warning of my presence. I turned a corner and looked straight into the sunset and up the Upper Bay. In the waning light the mountains had grown to twice their size and darkened to a royal blue . . . the sky was ablaze with the dying sun and a couple of loons softly yodeled to each other in the shallows of the tidal zone between the islands. The coyote picked up the call and his yips carried across the island to be answered by others until the atmosphere throbbed with the odd, spine-tingling yips and yelps of about half a dozen coyotes. In the half light the mountains crowded in and

courtesy of the National Park Service

grew taller and some islands which sat on the water within the great circle of mountains beckoned with an air of mystery that was irresistible.

Margaret Piggott

A baleen whale, the humpback whale uses baleen plates, its mouth opening, tongue, and ventral grooves, to feed. The baleen plates are very coarse and have a composition similar to that of human fingernails. The inside edges of the plates end in coarse bristles that are similar in appearance to matted goat hair. . . . The ventral grooves or pleats in the chin of the humpback extend from the lips, or mandible, two-thirds of the way down the body. (Using the human body for comparison, the pleats would run from the lips to the knees.) The pleated throat expands to allow the humpback to engulf huge quantities of water and feed (krill). When the mouth is shut, the feed is contained by the matted inner surface of the baleen and the water is expelled through this matting and the spaces between the plates. . . . A humpback whale can open its mouth 90 degrees, and when its mouth is agape and its pleated throat is distended, the story of Jonah is suddenly very believable.

Charles Jurasz[7]

when another animal makes its appearance. If a polite conversation does not settle the issue, a hard fluke-slapping of the water's surface when the animals are within a mile or so of one another may do the job.

But if the interloper persists, a full-bodied or impact breach, with the entire body out of the water, will make the statement. An animal may repeat the jump to advertise his stamina as well as his displeasure. The interloper may respond in a similar manner, or may simply back down by changing course or swimming through, staying close to the surface instead of making feeding dives. The arguments fall off as the animals distribute themselves amongst the feed while establishing a kind of pecking (or breaching) order.

Charles Jurasz[8]

One of the largest concentrations of harbor seals in Southeast Alaska is found within Glacier Bay. In 1978, for example, over 4400 seals were counted in Johns Hopkins and Muir Inlets, where the seals congregate in spring and summer to give birth to their pups on the icebergs discharged from tidewater glaciers.

Seals clearly prefer icebergs for pupping, presumably because of the protection from predators they afford. But the evidence of glacial history suggests

One frequently witnessed pattern in spring . . . establishes feeding areas or territories.
A single animal, or pair, may have just come into an area and begun feeding

that they may have been forced to pup on land for extensive periods in the last several thousand years, as do the great majority of harbor seals in the North Pacific Rim today. Just two centuries ago, glacial ice excluded seals from Glacier Bay completely, and since then, availability of iceberg concentrations in the bay has fluctuated. Recently the seals have benefited from conditions in Glacier Bay, but they may be facing a very stressful period within the next decade or two if, as seems likely, recession of Muir Glacier greatly reduces iceberg concentrations in upper Muir Inlet.

That seals have been accustomed to pupping on land is suggested by certain facets of their behavior. Young pups and their mothers typically show a surprising lack of coordination in maintaining contact with each other. Should they become separated, they search in a frantic but haphazard manner, which not infrequently fails to bring the two back together. This behavior may have evolved in response to a stable terrestrial shoreline, but is ill-adapted to the complex, shifting shoreline presented by the icepack. Separation is probably not unusual under natural conditions; the crying of lost pups was heard frequently during the study. Human interference at this tenuous time has the potential to greatly aggravate the problem.

Seals, secure in the fastness of their icepack, are often not alert to their surroundings, and often are badly startled by the unexpected approach of a person or machine. This can precipitate a crash dive without the opportunity for mother/pup coordination; the consequent separation may result in starvation of the pup. Even a quiet approach, by a boat of any type, usually results in seals vacating their bergs, often hastily.

Greg Streveler[9]

The whole area from Dry Bay to Icy Point is dominated by the snowy peak of Mount Fairweather . . . some 15,300 feet high. Its appearance gives promise of calm seas or warns of storms, and it is therefore called "the paddler's mountain" by the natives.

Frederica de Laguna[10]

In all the splendor of the drenched sunlight, straight out of the violet sparkling sea, rose the magnificent peaks of the Fairweather Range and towered against the sky. No great snow mountains rising from the land have ever affected me as did that long and noble chain glistening out of the sea.

Ella Higginson, 1908

We had already visited the head of . . . [Lituya] bay, which is perhaps the most extraordinary place in the world. To form an idea of it, it is necessary to conceive a basin of water, unfathomable in the middle, bordered by peaked mountains, of great height, covered with snow, and without one blade of grass to decorate this vast heap of rocks, condemned by nature to eternal sterility. I never beheld the surface of the water ruffled by a single breath of wind. Nothing disturbs it but the fall of enormous masses of ice, which frequently separate from five different glaciers, while the sound is re-echoed by the distant mountains.

Jean François de Galáup,
Comte de Lapérouse, 1786

At the entrance of this harbour perished twenty-one brave seamen. Reader, whoever thou art, mingle thy tears with ours.

. . . On the 13th of July [1786], three boats departed at five in the morning, to place the soundings on the plan that had been drawn of the bay. They were commanded by Mr. d'Escures, lieutenant of a man of war and knight of St. Lewis. Mr. de la Pérouse had given him written instruction, expressly prohibiting him from approaching the current; but at the moment when he thought himself at a distance from it, he was drawn into it. Messrs. de la Borde, two brothers, and Mr. de Flassan, who were in the boat of the second frigate, hesitated

"Naufrage des Deux Chaloupes, Au Port Des Francais" by M. Ozanne courtesy of the Anchorage Historical and Fine Arts Museum

not to expose their own lives, to assist their comrades. But, alas! they only shared their fate. The third boat was under the command of Mr. Boutin, lieutenant of a man of war. This officer, bravely struggling against the breakers, made vain but useless attempts to assist his friends for some hours, and would have perished likewise, but for the superior construction of his boat [and] his enlightened prudence. . . . The Indians appeared to participate in our grief, which is extreme. Affected, but not discouraged, by our misfortune, we departed the 30th of July, to continue our voyage.

From an inscription buried
on Cenotaph Island by Lapérouse

The Tlingit endowed all nature with spirit life, and so accounted for the many mysteries that compassed them about. . . . The legend of Lituya tells of a monster of the deep who dwells in the ocean caverns near the entrance. He is known as Kah Lituya, "the Man of Lituya." He resents any approach to his domain, and all

of those whom he destroys become his slaves, and take the form of bears, and from their watch towers on the lofty mountains of the Mt. Fairweather range they herald the approach of canoes, and with their master they grasp the surface water and shake it as if it were a sheet, causing tidal waves to rise and engulf the unwary.

George Emmons, 1911

Giant waves have brought chaos to Lituya Bay at least three times since Lapérouse. But the most recent was the worst, July 9,1958. Weather clear, water calm. At 9:00 P.M. the troller *Badger* entered the Bay and dropped anchor near another troller, the *Sunmore*. The sun was setting, the tide ebbing. At 10:16 the Fairweather fault, which runs directly through Gilbert and Crillon Inlets at the rear of the Bay, was wrenched in a violent earthquake. One minute later ninety million tons of rock with a displacement of forty million cubic yards plummeted from the northeast wall of Gilbert Inlet into the Bay.

adapted from Dave Bohn[11]

"Hang on!" Bill yelled. I clung to him. We pitched and tossed, bounced like matchsticks, from one side of the deck to the other.

Bill fought his way to the wheel and started the engine. "Hang on!" he yelled again. Directly ahead and thundering toward us, was what seemed to be a mile-high wall of water.

Bill threw the throttle wide open and pointed the *Badger* into the roaring avalanche. Our one slim hope of survival required riding the wave. The anchor jerked loose, whipped freakishly in midair, then gouged into the pilothouse. We tossed and pitched, riding upward into the wave. High, higher, higher.

Miraculously, we reached the peak of the wave without capsizing. Battered and bruised, I crawled to peep over the deck. The world was crazy. Acres of tangled trees, their roots grotesque and askew, crashed and churned the water. In horror, I watched the

Sunmore roll over and disappear.

During the nightmare, Bill fought for control of the *Badger* as we were pushed wildly seaward. Finally, the wave heaved, and we were pitched far out into the Gulf of Alaska. That driving force moved on and we were left tossing in an angry sea.

Hours later, adrift in our tiny skiff, the *Badger* gone, we saw a searchlight and heard a motor. Over here! Over here!

Vi Swanson Kreutzer[12]

This stream is the wildest I have ever seen; there is scarcely a one-hundred-yard stretch of fair water anywhere along its course. Running with an eight- to ten-knot current, and aggravated by rocky points, sharp bends and immense boulders, the stream is also rendered dangerous by the innumerable rapids and eddies which disturb its surface.

We are now brought into actual contact with the giant ice-fields of Alaska. A pass several miles in width cuts at right angles the range of mountains which runs along the eastern shore of the Alsek, in the valley of which lies an immense glacier; and between this and the stream is an old moraine, a wild, uneven, stony area.

All this part of the country is suggestive of violence; these colossal heaps of rock rudely hurled from the mountain heights, the roaring and thundering of the internal forces of the glacier and moraine, whole forests laid low by the fury of the tempests; the wild, angry torrent of the Alsek River, roaring as it sweeps past the desolate scenes — a combination framed by nature to be inimical to life. These monstrous piles of rugged rock and mass of cavernous and blackened ice seemed formed to harbor in their weird fastnesses hobgoblins in some form of life. Numerous water-courses drain this glacier and moraine, threading their courses among the stony waste and tunneling beneath the ice, they rush along to swell the volume of the Alsek River.

E. J. Glave, 1890

SITKA NATIONAL HISTORICAL PARK

From-place-of-tidal-waters-people . . .

At Sitka cultural conflict, fueled by greed, caused tragedy. The proud civilization of the Tlingit Indians clashed with Russian expansion and exploitation. But there was also reconciliation, exemplified by a Russian priest and the Indian converts who accepted his vision. This park commemorates Tlingit culture and the Russian experience in America.

The story of Russian America is similar to other chapters in the book of frontier imperialism. Freebooters cross a sea or a continent and, in places remote from authority, lay waste the country and its people. When authorities in the distant capital — be it St. Petersburg or Washington, Madrid or London — hear of rapacity and cruelty on the frontier, they send officers and missionaries to stop injustice. Given some success in these efforts, the original people and the colonists may reach accommodation. Sitka symbolizes this evolution as it affected the Tlingits of southeast Alaska.

Russian expansion eastward across Siberia to North America followed the lure of furs. Most precious of these was the pelt of the sea otter — abundant along the Alaska coast from the Aleutian Islands to the Tlingit homeland in the Sitkan Islands. During the last half of the 18th Century, the Russians, commanding Aleut hunters, killed off the sea otters in Alaska's western reaches. Seeking new hunting grounds, they moved eastward to Kodiak Island and Prince William Sound. From these advanced bases they probed the southeast coast, encountering the Kolosh, as the Russians called the Tlingits, from Yakutat Bay southward.

They found an able and resolute people. Through practical skills — fishing, hunting, building — the Tlingits had mastered their rich environment. They produced tools, ornaments, and ceremonial regalia for trade with nations beyond the coastal mountains and across the seas. These formal and closely guarded trade relationships brought surplus wealth distributed in ritual potlatches by Tlingit clans and societies. Inheritors of highly developed spiritual and esthetic

traditions, they were an organized and imperious people.

Before the Russians came, the Tlingits had had only sporadic contact with European explorers — British, French, and Spanish. In accounts of their voyages the Europeans noted the large villages and the strength and temper of the Tlingit people. They counselled future visitors to deal cautiously with them. And they began trading arms for Tlingit furs.

The Tsar's agent in Alaska was Aleksandr Baranov. As chief manager of the Russian-American Company, he ran the fur trade and the government in Russian America. Alarmed by growing competition from foreign traders and the threat of firearms in Tlingit hands, Baranov moved to assert Russian control in southeast Alaska. In 1799 he established a trading post just north of present Sitka. Its troubled history ended three years later when Tlingit warriors from several clans attacked and destroyed the fort. Insult, treachery, and uncontrolled competition between the Russians and other traders had pushed the Tlingits to violence.

Baranov knew that he had to reassert Russian supremacy in southeast Alaska or lose its riches to British traders and aggressive Yankees. In 1804 he mobilized an army and a fleet at Kodiak and sailed for Sitka Sound. Backed by guns of the frigate *Neva,* he demanded that the Tlingits evacuate their village and fort at Sitka. Their refusal precipitated battle. After attack and counterattack and pounding from naval guns, the Tlingits — their ammunition exhausted — abandoned Sitka. Baranov, though wounded in a charge, immediately turned his men to the task of building the settlement of New Archangel, soon to be the capital of Russian America.

As years went by, enmity and distrust between Russians and Tlingits subsided. Social and economic interdependence in the isolated colony helped ease the strains of conflict. And in time, the Russian Orthodox Church, through the work of the priest Ivan Veniaminov, further bound together the fate of the two peoples. The

Tsar charged the Church with two responsibilities: religious guidance of the Russian colonists, who were in dire need of moral discipline, and conversion and education of the Native people, who accepted the Church, at first grudgingly, as an improvement over the rougher ministrations of the fur traders. Veniaminov, later Bishop Innocent of Kamchatka and all Alaska, contributed greatly to the change from conflict to civility in Russian America.

The Sitka parkland preserves some of the settings, structures, and artifacts recalling this history — from traditional Tlingit times through the Russian period. In memorializing the Tlingit people and the Russian venture in Alaska, Sitka illustrates larger themes both historical and modern. From the first arrival of Europeans, and on to the present day, cultural confrontations have threatened Alaska's Native societies. Their struggle to perpetuate key elements of traditional life in the flux of intrusive change has met with mixed success. Today that struggle continues — centered on the land and the revival of traditional values and skills. Rifts between the Native people and later arrivals also continue. Enlightenment and good will are needed as much now as they were in an earlier era. ∎

The name Tlingit was bestowed by the neighboring Tsimshian Indians. It means "from-place-of-tidal-waters-people."

William L. Paul, Sr.

He was dressed in a much more superb style than any chief we had hitherto seen on this coast, and he supported a degree of state consequence. . . . His external robe was a very fine large garment, that reached from his neck down to his heels, made of wool from the mountain sheep, neatly variegated with several colours, and edged, and otherwise decorated with little tufts, or frogs of woollen yarn, dyed of various colours. . . . The whole exhibited a magnificent

drawing by JoAnn George from *"Carved History"*, © copyright 1980 by the Alaska Natural History Association

appearance, and indicated a taste for dress and ornament, that we had not supposed the natives of these regions to possess.

Capt. George Vancouver, 1794[1]

Senator Charles Sumner, having pored over the accounts of explorers and ethnographers, described the Tlingit people in these words during the debates leading to the purchase of Alaska by the United States in 1867:

They are of constant courage. As daring navigators they are unsurpassed, sailing six or seven hundred miles in their open canoes. Some are thrifty, and show a sense of property. Some have developed an aptitude for trade unknown to their northern neighbors or to the Indians of the United States. . . . Their superior nature discards corporal punishment, even for boys, as an ignominy not to be endured. They believe in a Creator and in the immortality of the soul. But here a mystic fable is woven into their faith. The spirits of heroes dead in battle are placed in the sky and appear in the Aurora Borealis.

There is now no one at Nootka [Vancouver Island], neither Englishman nor Spaniard. It has been left tenantless; when they reappear there, they will endeavor to extend their trade and found settlements in our direction.

Aleksandr Baranov, 1800

The Kolosh chiefs came into our tent and complained against our hunters, using many rude and insolent expressions, accusing them of always causing outrages, robbing the chattels placed with the dead, etc. . . . In addition they said that we hunted furs in their waters causing them to suffer great shortages in clothing and other necessities for which they barter with the Europeans. I tried to justify ourselves and our hunters without success; I tried to mollify them with gifts and tobacco but it was hopeless. I did not show my vexation with their rudeness and insolence, but they showed their intention of severing peaceful and friendly ties with us.

[Then followed bloody battle, taking of hostages, and peace negotiations.]

Although these promises seemed extremely doubtful, we had many reasons to accept them in order to quiet the animosity of these people and keep it from spreading further along the coast, and also because we didn't have enough defensive weapons and shot, we decided to leave their punishment to a more suitable opportunity when their last assurances prove to be lies.

I. Kuskov to Baranov, 1802

B 62.1.776; courtesy of the Anchorage Historical and Fine Arts Museum

Aleut hunting brigades of up to 30 baidarkas paddled to sea otter feeding grounds, sometimes many miles from the coast. There they spread out in a line, just in sight of each other, and waited. When a sea otter surfaced and was sighted, a paddle was raised. The silent signal went down the line. The baidarkas circled the spot and the hunters closed in, killing the animal with bows and arrows. One hunting foray might yield hundreds of skins.

On the 1st of October [1804] four of the ships were drawn up in line before the enemy's fort . . . .

Mistaking . . . inaction for timidity, Baranof rashly ordered his men to carry the fort by storm. He was met by the savages in a compact body, and a well-directed fire was opened on his men, causing a stampede among the [Aleuts], who were dragging along the guns. Left with a mere handful of sailors and promyshleniki, the commander was forced to retire. The Kolosh then rushed forth in pursuit. . . . [The Russian] retreat was covered by the guns of the flotilla, but for which circumstance it is probable that none would have escaped . . . .

The following day Lisianski was requested by [the wounded] Baranof to take charge of the expedition. He at once opened a brisk fire on the fort. . . . hostages were delivered into the hands of the Russians . . . evacuation of the fort was demanded . . . .

Hubert Howe Bancroft[2]

I recommenced my fire, believing they were merely protracting the time till a reinforcement should arrive. . . . During the day we took two large canoes, one of which belonged to the old man . . . I advised him to go back and persuade his countrymen to evacuate the fort as soon as possible, if they valued their safety. . . .

When morning came, I observed a great number of crows hovering about the settlement. I sent on shore to ascertain the cause of this; and the messenger returned with the news that the natives had quitted the fort during the night. . . .

It was on the 8th that the fate of Sitca fort was decided. After everything that could be of use was removed out of it, it was burned to the ground.

Urey Lisianski, commander
of the *Neva*, 1804

From the kind treatment received from the Governor [Baranov], I was induced to form a very favorable opinion of him. He was sixty-five years of age, and had spent the last eighteen years of his life at different stations on the coast, in the capacity of agent and officer of the Russian American Company, — excluded, as it were, from all civilized society, except that of a few of his fellow-adventurers. He possessed a strong mind, easy manners and deportment, and was apparently well fitted for the place he filled. He commanded the greatest respect from the Indians, who regarded him with mingled feelings of love and fear.

Capt. John D'Wolf, 1805[3]

I asked Mr. Baranof how the directors could neglect to send surgeons to a country the climate of which was conducive to all kinds of diseases, and where men may at any time be wounded . . . and need surgical treatment. "I do not know," he said, "whether the directors trouble themselves to think about it; but we doctor ourselves a little, and if a man is wounded so as to require an operation, he must die."

Capt. Vasilii Golovinn, 1810

The aborigines of America . . . are not subjects of Russia in the same sense as the aborigines of Siberia and the intervening islands. They do not exhibit that badge of servitude which, having been introduced by the earliest conquerors, has travelled eastward from the Gulf of Finland to Behring's Straits.

Sir George Simpson, 1841

In spite of how well I became acquainted with the Tlingit and how friendly our intercourse was, a long period of time passed before they were satisfied as to my knowledge and ability. . . .

In general [the Kolosh converts] fulfill their obligations to the church quite well. They always attend church when they can . . . and willingly listen to instruction. . . . The activity and industry characteristic of all the Kolosh may serve as an example to others, and their orderly lives may inspire conviction in their Kolosh brethren.

The Sitka Seminary had a great influence on the future of the American Mission, an influence that remains to this day and which kept Orthodox Catholicism alive among the Aleutians and the Indians through some very trying times to the present. Its students were Aleutians, Koloshi, and members of other Alaskan Indian tribes who were to carry on the work of teaching and propagating the Orthodox Catholic Faith in America.

Bishop Innocent

. . . the Orthodox tradition maintains great respect for the language and culture of the individual. The Orthodox mission has traditionally used the language of the people. [Among the Aleut, Yupik, and Tlingit] use of the vernacular was encouraged. . . . In other words, there is no attack in Orthodoxy on the basic worth of the individual. There is no attack on a person's language. Rather, the Church sought to instill a sense of pride in the Native language and foster popular literacy in it.

Richard Dauenhauer[4]

"Captain Pestchourof ordered the Russian flag hauled down, and thereby, with brief declaration, transferred and delivered the territory of Alaska to the United States; the garrisons and our men of war fired the international salute; a brief reply of acceptance was made as the stars and stripes were run up and similarly saluted, and we stood upon the soil of the United States."

Thus, without further ceremony, without even banqueting or speech-making, this vast area of land, belonging by right to neither, was transferred from one European race to the offshoot of another.

Hubert Howe Bancroft

It is a straggling, peaceful sort of a town, edging along shore at the foot of high mountains, and sheltered from the surge and turmoil of the ocean by a sea-wall of rocky, pine-covered islands. The moss has grown greener and thicker on the roofs of the solid old wooden houses that are relics of Russian days . . . .

Eliza Ruhamah Scidmore, 1883

I thought of this poem
when I felt my pride with the group. . . .
As a man stands on earth
he has only two reasons
for being here:
      living and dying.
            And whatever comes between
                  is just a form of being remembered.

                  And that's
                  why I'm here
                  is to be remembered
                        as a Tlingit
                              and that's where my pride is
                                    is being a Tlingit Indian.

John Bell[5]

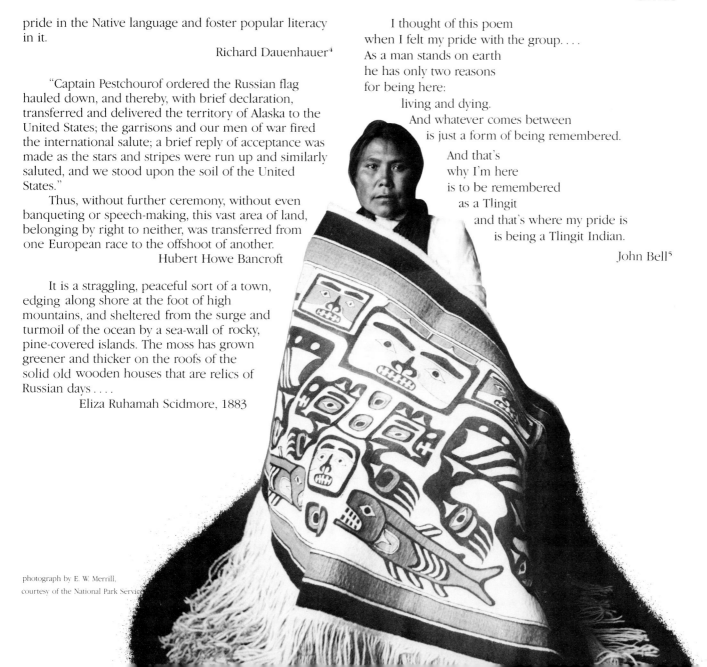

photograph by E. W. Merrill,
courtesy of the National Park Service

A stampede unequalled in history . . .

It was a nation down on its luck when the cry "Gold! Gold in the Klondike!" rang forth in 1897. Depression and frontier's end had broken the pace of progress. The notion that Americans were somehow exempt from the toils of fate and history began to fade as the century wore to a close.

Tales of the "great big land up yonder" had appeared in the popular press for decades. Gold had been taken from Alaska and the Yukon for 20 years. Trails had been blazed and ships crowded Pacific Coast ports. But the great stampede awaited the moment when Kondike fever and national frustration broke over the dam together.

Then ensued an adventure that revived lagging spirits — an epic that filled attics and museums with letters and lore, and in time made heroes of argonauts who repeated the tales of those splendid days to youngsters. They, in their turn, would retrace the historic trails.

Surging crowds fought for passage at Seattle, Portland, San Francisco. Classy ships and condemned rust buckets competed for the traffic. They sailed low in the water, packed from keel to rigging with stampeders who jauntily waved straw hats as they steamed north to the unknown, but surely to glory.

Through the island-protected Inside Passage, they came, descending on the tent towns of Dyea and Skagway in swirling mobs. There a scene of chaos and opportunity awaited. Runners hawked their patrons' wares and handed out cards for every kind of business and pleasure. Innocent, enthusiastic, and unprepared, many goldseekers fell prey to con men and bunco artists, fleeced of their purses and packs before the first step on the trail.

Survivors of these initiations toted their goods over the coastal ranges on the Chilkoot and White Pass trails. Indian packers helped some. Others pooled their cash to buy horses and dogs. In time, enterprisers built trams and wagon roads and, eventually, a railroad over White Pass.

In fact, miners already in the country had swarmed to the gold fields near the junction of the Klondike and Yukon rivers. They had staked all claims before the end of 1896, soon after George Carmack and his brothers-in-law Skookum Jim and Tagish Charley washed the first $4 pan at Rabbit, now Bonanza, Creek. But the rush from outside that started in 1897 continued for many years. Primitive and rugged conditions of stampede days were symbolized by the line of pack-burdened hopefuls lock-stepping up the final icy crest of Chilkoot Trail, by the thousands of broken carcasses on Dead Horse Trail, by hastily fabricated rafts and boats breaking up in Yukon River rapids.

These anxious scenes and the lawlessness and boom-town character of Skagway changed rapidly. Commercial rates and ticketed passengers replaced the wild bidding and the hard scramble over rock and ice. Steamboats connected with the train at Whitehorse and safely warped around the rapids. Dyea faded entirely, for the train over White Pass killed the commerce of the Chilkoot Trail. By now both Skagway and the Klondike boom town Dawson had replaced tents and shacks with classic western architecture. The stampeders had moved on to other gold fields or gone home, except for a few who stayed on because they loved the country.

Almost that fast, the gold rush was over. These trails and towns lived with their memories and welcomed the tourists who kept the grand adventure alive. Today, historic Skagway and the old trails crossing into Canada's Yukon Territory preserve the ambience of that frenetic time. They still link the sea with Dawson and the Klondike. ∎

To Whom It May Concern

I do this day, locate and claim by right of discovery, five hundred feet running upstream from this notice. Located this 17th day of August, 1896.

G. W. Carmack

GOLD! GOLD! GOLD! GOLD!
68 RICH MEN ON THE
STEAMER PORTLAND — STACKS OF
YELLOW METAL!

At 3 o'clock this morning the steamer *Portland* from St. Michael for Seattle, passed up the Sound with more than a ton of solid gold aboard.

Seattle Post-Intelligencer
July 17, 1897

In an incredibly short space of time the inhabitants of the coast cities were beside themselves with excitement. "Coast Again Gold Crazy," was the Eastern comment. A stampede unequalled in history was on.

Tappan Adney, 1897

We are going to the Golden Klondyke to seek our fortune. Perhaps never to return, but time will tell how we shall fare.

J. A. McRae, February 1898

·J. H. BROOKS, The Largest Pack .. Trains in Alaska.

The Old Reliable

PACKER AND FREIGHTER

From Skagway to Lake Bennett, Atlin
and Intermediate Points.

PROMPT AND SAFE DELIVERY OF GOODS GUARANTEED.

Office, Brannick Hotel, Bond Street, **Skagway, Alaska.**

Klondike memorabilia courtesy of the Clarence L. Andrews Collection, University of Alaska, Fairbanks

Rooms Single or en Suite
With or Withour Bath

Hot and Cold Water
Electric Lights
Telephone

The Pullen House

ONE BLOCK FROM POST OFFICE

Alaska's Most Famous Tourist Hotel

FAMOUS FOR ITS HOME COOKING
Milk, Butter, Cottage Cheese from our own Dairy

Rooms, $1.50 and up
Meals, $1.00

MRS. H. S. PULLEN, Prop.
SKAGWAY, ALASKA

I fully expect before many years to see a pack trail through . . . [White Pass], followed by a wagon road, and I would not be at all surprised to see a railroad through to the lakes.

Capt. William Moore, 1887

Based on this expectation, Captain Moore homesteaded at the mouth of the Skagway River, built a sawmill and wharf, and waited for the gold rush. Moore's vision became reality in the summer of 1897.

We have learned already to place no reliance upon any person's word. Everyone seems to have lost his head, and cannot observe or state facts.

The very horses and animals partake of the fever and are restless . . . . Accidents and runaways are occurring every few moments.

Tappan Adney, 1897

The beach had . . . become a human anthill, a confused melee of swearing men and neighing horses, of rasping saws and sputtering campfires, of creaking wagons and yelping dogs — a jungle of tents and sheet-iron stoves and upturned boats scattered between the mountainous piles of goods and hay.

Atop these sprawling heaps, knee deep in flour

sacks and frying pans, perspiring men bawled out the names on every outfit and tossed them down to the waiting owners. . . .

Above the beach, in the forested flatland, the town of Skagway was still taking shape, a shifting and ever changing mélange of shacks and tents, crammed with men frantic to get over the trail and into the Klondike before freeze-up.

Pierre Berton[1]

I have stumbled upon a few tough corners of the globe during my wandering beyond the outposts of civilization, but I think the most outrageously lawless quarter I ever struck was Skagway. . . .

Alexander MacDonald, 1897

At the first rush the bunco men and gamblers and prostitutes got in and became organized, and controlled matters pretty much their own way. . . . Matters came to a head early in July, when a returning Klondiker was robbed of his dust in open day. The people were aroused, and they determined to endure it no longer. . . . [The death of Soapy Smith and the rout of his gang] . . . was a self-purification. Skagway and Dyea are now models of good order.

Annual Report of the
Governor of the District
of Alaska, 1898

Skagway and Dawson were products of the same Gold Rush, but they were vastly different in character. Skagway was lawless and disorderly and wicked in those early years, and the Stroller remembers it as being very grim as well. The town was full of gold-seekers grimly determined to get to the Klondike, and with a multitude of others who were just as grimly determined to relieve the gold-seekers of a part of their burdens, particularly the cash portions thereof.

Dawson was far — sometimes very far — from being a model for the Young People's Society of

Christian Endeavor, but there was a gayety and lightheartedness about its sinning that was absent in Skagway. And while Dawson provided plenty of places and opportunities for the suckers to dispose of their money, the suckers were never steered, dragooned and bootjacked into these places as they had been at

Skagway. In Dawson, also, the Royal Northwest Mounted Police maintained a surprising degree of law and order considering the number of people congregated there and the kind of people many of them were.

Stroller White, 1898

We left Dyea on July 12 at noon, to walk the dreaded trail of 42 miles over the Chilkoot Pass to Lake Bennett. . . . With staff in hand, at last I had taken my place in that continuous line of pushing humans and straining animals. Before me, behind me, abreast of me almost every man toted a pack of 60 to 80 pounds, in addition to driving dogs and horses harnessed to sleighs and carts, herding pack ponies and the odd cow, while one woman drove an ox-cart.

Martha Black, July 1898[2]

After the Indian had left us, Stacey and I viewed our hundreds of pounds of supplies with much concern, especially when we saw the steep, slippery trail leading from the river up the canyon. We knew we would have to make a number of back-breaking relay trips to establish our first cache. Quickly, we began dividing our supplies, making about sixty-five to seventy-pound packs for each. Then we started. The trail immediately crooked up, narrow and slippery. As we climbed, we threw our weight toward the inside of the trail, hugging the precipitous walls. The fact that we must make several trips over this trail for the rest of our supplies was hard to bear.

Ed Lung, May 1897

That six miles of canyon cost us nearly everything but our shirts. It was one grand splash, slide, and tumble. Horses going down all along the trail. Ours went down off and on. Once, all three were down at the same time. . . .

courtesy of the Historical Photography Collection, University of Washington Libraries

Some enterprising fellows had seen a Klondike right there. They had begun improving the trail by bridging ravines and corduroying bogs, charging tolls to those who crossed, and that meant everyone. It was impossible to go any other way.

Robert Medill, September 1897

On our way to Sheep's Camp we were overtaken by an ox-team the owner of which lifted little Emily and placed her on the loaded wagon, which gave her quite a rest.

There were so few children on the trail that our little girl attracted a great deal of attention and every one had a smile for her. One day a man said, "God bless you dear, you are just the size of my little girl at home," and tears sprang to his eyes as he pathetically spoke of his child.

Louella Craig, February 1898

Tents, shacks, shanties and buildings of varied shape, size and hue were crowded along either side of the road which follows the narrow ravine towards the pass. Thousands of people of all ages and nationalities, women as well as men, were camped here. Throngs of adventurous gold seekers were moving hither and thither in every direction, surging over snow drifts or along the narrow, winding and picturesque streets, with heavy packs, or tugging away in a persevering endeavor to drag their heavily laden sleds towards the summit.

John Clum, Sheep Camp, April 1898

The first two miles above Sheep Camp bring one to the scales, a point 2195 feet higher than the former, and this portion of the route is conceded to be the worst and most laborious of the trail to the summit. . . . The scales mark the point at which goods are weighed previous to being taken from here to the summit, the charges for transport by packing from this point upward being very much in excess to prior ones. . . .

Sgt. Yanert, March 1898

When about a mile from the summit we came into full view of it, and I just halted and gazed, for it surely is the sight of a lifetime . . . . A short distance farther on we passed over the snow slide under which no one knows how many poor fellows are still buried and won't know till the snow melts.

Harley Tuck, April 1898

Now we are at Chilkoot Pass. . . . Many lose their gold fever here and return home and many have turned back before reaching this point. It is blowing hard today and the weather is somewhat dark, so not as many are going up today as in bright weather. . . .

We now divide our load and each puts his pack on his back. The sled must also be carried. When one looks up only and not down and is careful about his footsteps he gets along above all expectations. The grade is so steep that one's pack bumps the one ahead when we walk close together. . . .

B. Harsted, March 1898

. . . it is about as fatiguing a climb as could well be imagined. Without exaggeration I should say the angle must be about 45 degrees. . . . By dint of stolid plodding, with an occasional pause to take breath, we reached the summit.

Julius Price, June 1898

Packed our load to the summit. We climbed in snow all the way. The summit is a "corker"!

Ed Lung, June 1897

Well, Azora, here I am on top of the mountain and will just sit down long enough to write you a line. It is a beautiful day. The sun shines bright, and I can see down to Lake Linderman on one side and looking back the other way it is a sight to behold away back to Dyea. The trail as far as one can see is just lined with people. You never saw anything like it. I would just like to have a picture of it and send you. Mountains on all sides all covered with snow. It is only about 1/2 mile from where I am to where we drove with our oxen. Have got most all of our stuff up as far as we can drive. Now we have got to carry it up here on our backs just like going up stairs, but you ought to see them slide down. All one has to do is to sit down and away they go. That part of it is fun, but I tell you one never knows what work is until he begins to carry goods up here. Some carry one hundred lbs. at a time, but most everyone only carrys 50 lbs. I wish Louis was here for a few minutes, just long enough to slide down once. I guess the snow must be about twenty feet deep.

Martin Howard, February 1898

Skagway interests promoted the White Pass Trail as superior to the Chilkoot, boasting that pack animals would encounter no difficulty in crossing from tidewater to Lake Bennett. Despite this claim, the route soon earned the name, Dead Horse Trail.

The trail along the bed of the river is a continuous mire, knee-deep to men and horses. Here and there is a spot where a spring branch crosses the trail, and in such spots, which are twenty to thirty feet across, there is simply no bottom. One such hole is beside our camp. Of the first train of five horses and three men that I saw go by, three horses and two men got in, and with difficulty got out. After that every horse went in to his tail in the mud, but, after desperate struggles, got upon solid ground.

There is no common interest. The selfish are crowding on, every man for himself. Unless something is done soon the trail will be blocked, and then no one will get through.

Tappan Adney, 1897

Such a scene of havoc and destruction . . . can scarcely be imagined. Thousands of packhorses lie dead along the way, sometimes in bunches under the cliffs, with pack-saddles and packs where they have fallen from the rock above, sometimes in tangled masses filling the mud-holes and furnishing the only footing for our poor pack animals on the march — often, I regret to say, exhausted but still alive, a fact we are unaware of until after the miserable wretches turn beneath the hoofs of our cavalcade. The eyeless sockets of the pack animals everywhere account for the myriads of ravens along the road. The inhumanity which this trail has been witness to, the heartbreak and suffering which so many have undergone, cannot be imagined. They certainly cannot be described.

Maj. J. M. Walsh, Royal
Canadian Mounted Police, retired,
October 1897

In April 1898, engineer C. E. Hawkins arrived in Skagway to build the railroad over White Pass. Lacking surveys, plans, and equipment, he recalled " . . . there was simply the White Pass, rising terrible and adamant, buried in deep snow drifts, defying entrance to civilization, and its ally, transportation."

The dangerous, difficult work went ahead anyway.

At Mile 11 two men were crushed beneath an enormous granite boulder. "Leave it be," Mike Heney said of the immovable rock. "It's as fitting a monument as any driller would want to have."

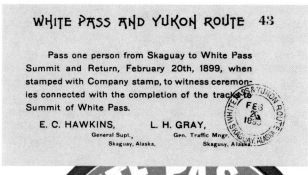

WHITE PASS AND YUKON ROUTE 43

Pass one person from Skaguay to White Pass Summit and Return, February 20th, 1899, when stamped with Company stamp, to witness ceremonies connected with the completion of the track to Summit of White Pass.

E. C. HAWKINS,   L. H. GRAY,
General Supt.,   Gen. Traffic Mngr.,
Skaguay, Alaska.   Skaguay, Alaska.

WHITE PASS & YUKON ROUTE

GATEWAY TO THE YUKON

MADE IN U.S.A.

The many difficult engineering problems of building a railroad to the interior of Alaska have been solved, and the White Pass & Yukon railroad is now completed and in operation from Skagway over the summit. Its construction is a marvel, the acme of engineering skill, the triumph of capital and labor in subduing and making subservant to man the heretofore impassable and barren vastness created by God, formerly preserved for Himself as it were, and visited only by the howling blasts of Boreas.

Skagway Guide, 1898

On the summit we found typical March weather: snow, ice, water, mud, slush, fog and chill. The fog prevented us from getting a view down toward the Klondike country, 600 miles away. The British flag and the Stars and Stripes were floating side by side on the provisional boundary line between Alaska and British Columbia, and several Canadian police were on duty there. . . .

At the time of our visit the railroad terminus was at the summit of the pass, from which point passengers bound for the Klondike were transported to Lake Bennett by sleighs. The deep snow was melting so rapidly and slumping so badly that the sled loads of people and grain we saw depart for the Upper Yukon were, we were told, the last to get through until the completion of the railroad to Bennett.

John Burroughs, 1899

There is a land of pure delight,
Where grass grows belly high,
Where horses don't sink out of sight,
We'll reach it by-and-by.

blazed on a tree
by a Klondiker

Klondike memorabilia courtesy of the Clarence L. Andrews Collection, University of Alaska, Fairbanks

KATMAI NATIONAL PARK & PRESERVE

Great brooding wild land . . .

The arc of 15 volcanoes lining Shelikof Strait opposite Kodiak Island makes Katmai one of the world's most intense volcanic centers. The great eruption of 1912 collapsed Mount Katmai, thrust up a massive lava plug in Novarupta's vent, and created the Valley of Ten Thousand Smokes. It was among the four largest volcanic events of recent history. Shaken by many minor eruptions since 1912, the visible landscape is like an immense lid perforated by mountainous pressure valves, some of them rising 7,000 feet above sea level. These volcanoes are the upper works of the pipes and conduits of the subsurface furnace that rims the entire Alaska coast. They regularly eject steam, ash, and lava — signals to scientists who roam the surface checking the gauges of this trembling terrain.

Volcanism brought Katmai to world attention. Following the 1912 eruption the National Geographic Society sponsored scientific expeditions led by Dr. Robert F. Griggs. His accounts of volcanic phenomena and biologic devastation led to establishment in 1918 of Katmai National Monument, which at that time encompassed only the principal volcanic features and a narrow band of coastline. Since then Katmai has been enlarged repeatedly, the last time by the Alaska Lands Act of 1980. Today Katmai National Park and Preserve occupies most of the neck of the Alaska Peninsula — including an intricate Pacific coastline some 300 miles long, the volcanic heartland of the Aleutian Range, and the westside lake-and-river country and tundra plains. Thus, Katmai has become a transect through one of the earth's most important scientific, scenic, wildlife, and wilderness regions.

The coastal brown bear, largest predatory land mammal that yet roams the earth, finds its last big sanctuary in the Katmai region. These imposing creatures concentrate seasonally in the park and in neighboring state and federal refuges to feed along salmon spawning streams. At other times they disperse to wild pastures where they graze vegetation. In winter they withdraw to denning sites in the park's backcountry. Survivors of the Ice Age, these aloof but unpredictable giants recall boreal scenes familiar to the big-game hunters of ancient times.

Human occupation at Katmai dates back many thousands of years. At Brooks River, the connecting link between Naknek and Brooks lakes, ancient tools and house pits have allowed archeologists to trace the evolution of fishing and hunting cultures that found abundance along this biological funnel. For human predators, as for bears, the Brooks River falls have been a boon. As salmon press upstream toward spawning grounds, the falls hold them back. Waiting the chance to leap the barrier, perhaps injured or exhausted, they crowd the downstream pools and shallows, making easy prey.

Ash layers discovered during archeological digs at Brooks River record at least 12 volcanic events preceding the 1912 eruption. The oldest layer in the series dates to 5400 B.C. Other ash layers found in cores from the Gulf of Alaska carry the sequential record of Alaska volcanism back some 30,000 years.

The essence of Katmai is a forbidding wildness, stemming in part from the fresh evidence of volcanic cataclysm, in part from extremes of wind and weather, in part from the primordial relationship of the giant bears and the homing salmon. It seems a strange intersect in time and space, somehow inimical to all but very careful human exploration. Incredibly beautiful along the coast and in the lake country of bays and islands, it is yet a difficult landscape. Volcanic ash rises in choking clouds when winds howl through mountain passes. Accounts of travelers speak of quicksand and exhaustion, lack of good water, the lethal hazards of fording raging rivers, the quest for shelter in storms that envelope the region and last for days. The usual human superiority is challenged here, not with any focused intent, but with a grand indifference. Even more than the rumbling volcanoes and the looming bears, the silent persistence of the salmon symbolizes these

special qualities. They know no mercy, but in their cold perfection they have survived all attrition through all the ages. The backcountry of Katmai, which is almost all of it, places a person far back in time. The ear is cocked, the eye scanning. The gust of wind may be a warning. ∎

Great brooding wild land. Your winds and storms and unceasing suddenness of wind and cloud and rain and storm and clearing. Wind. Always the wind.

But I remember a night when an almost-full moon rose over La Gorce in clear and windless sky. Naknek Lake was sixty miles of glass and that may not happen again for half a century.

Dave Bohn[1]

About noon, getting through the pass and down a little on the south side, of a sudden we saw the ocean. . . . Thrilling as it was to view again from the mountain heights the North Pacific after all the months since we had left it behind, of a truth it looked dreary enough. It was a forbidding coast, with high, dark mountains and deep valleys hung over with clouds.

Josiah E. Spurr, 1898

The Savonoski River. Its headwaters are frozen — frozen rivers coming down from the volcanic summits. The Savonoski flows braided and it is not easy to keep track of the main channel. The valley is miles wide and flat, and the peaks surround. Moose and bear drift across the bars. Bald eagle flying high . . . watches. Lynx. Great grey owls. Cut-banks, sweepers, snags. Great Alaskan glacier-fed river, muddy. Easing across riffles and through eddies . . . a brown bear just stood up to see who but did not like the answer given by the wind.

Dave Bohn[2]

The Katmai Mountain blew up with lots of fire, and fire came down trail from Katmai with lots of smoke. We

B.78.180.24; courtesy of the Anchorage Historical and Fine Arts Museum

go fast Savonoski. Everybody get in bidarka. Helluva job. We come Naknek one day, dark, no could see. Hot ash fall. Work like hell.

American Pete, June 6, 1912

Two family arrived from Katmai scared and hungry and reported the volcanoes up 15 mile from Katmai to the left of Toscar trail and that 1/2 the hill blun up and covered up everything as far as they could see also that small rock were falling for 3 or 4 miles at sea but could not say more of it as everything es closed up with smoke . . . . No one es lost as far as they know but all the natives are east of Katmai and the main flow of smoke go there as a strong SW wind blowing so they are in a bad way.

C. L. Boudry, June 8, 1912

Kaflia Bay, June 9, 1912

My dear Wife Tania:

First of all I will let you know of our unlucky voyage. I do not know whether we shall be either alive or well. We are awaiting death at any moment. Of course do not be alarmed. A mountain has burst near here, so that we are covered with ashes, in some places 10 feet and 6 feet deep. All this began on the 6th of June. Night and day we light lamps. We cannot see the daylight. In a word it is terrible, and we are expecting death at any moment, and we have no water. All the rivers are covered with ashes. Just ashes mixed with water. Here are darkness and hell, thunder and noise. I do not know whether it is day or night. Vanka will tell you all about it. So kissing and blessing you both, good-bye. Forgive me. Perhaps we shall see each other again. God is merciful. Pray for us.

Your husband,
Ivan Orloff

The earth is trembling; it lightens every minute. It is terrible. We are praying.

The pearly-white pumice of the first eruption had hardly stopped cascading down the snow-covered mountainsides near Novarupta when from the same vent and from nearby fissures there issued a colossal volume of white-hot powdery ash. Within a few moments, no less than 2-1/2 cubic miles of ash were expelled, and the incandescent mass, acting like a fiery hot liquid, swept down the valley with incredible swiftness. Trees on the valleysides above the glowing avalanches were snapped off and carbonized by the scorching, tornadic wind. More than 40 square miles of the valley floor were buried beneath the ash, in places to a depth of 700 feet. No sooner had the glowing avalanches come to rest than hot gases, mostly steam derived from buried rivers and feeding springs, began to rise to the surface through myriads of small holes and cracks. . . .

At or about the same time . . . the entire top of Mount Katmai volcano, which lies 6 miles to the east, collapsed, leaving in place of its pointed peak a chasm almost 3 miles long and 2 miles wide. None can doubt that somewhere at depth the lava conduits under Katmai and Novarupta are connected, for although almost all of the ash and pumice issued from Novarupta, it was the top of Katmai that was engulfed.

Garland Curtis[3]

Mt. Katmai expedition. Photo by D. B. Church courtesy of the National Geographic Society

The sight that flashed into view as we surmounted the hillock was one of the most amazing visions ever beheld by mortal eye. The whole valley as far as the eye could reach was full of hundreds, no thousands — literally, tens of thousands — of smokes curling up from its fissured floor.

From our position they looked as small as the little fumaroles near by, but realizing something of their distance we knew many of them must be gigantic. Some were sending up columns of steam which rose a thousand feet before dissolving.

Robert F. Griggs, 1916[4]

No later visitors can ever experience the sensations that came over us as we prepared to camp for the first time within [the Valley's] confines. They will know in advance that it is safe, but we could not tell what dangers might lurk in its fumaroles.

Our feeling of admiration soon gave way to one of stupefaction. We were overawed. For a while we could neither think nor act in normal fashion.

It was a situation calculated to instill dread . . .

Robert F. Griggs, 1917[5]

Then an endless night on the hot, moisture-teeming ground; an endless rolling from side to side to escape the torment of the penetrating heat that seeped up from the hot, sodden ground; and always, as I looked down the Valley through the open tent door, shone the marble-like steam columns, which like tall, writhing specters, swayed in the dim twilight. . . .

Pictures cannot bring back the Valley of the Smokes. They have lost the awesomeness that lies in the setting. You may build in memory, but never reproduce the scenes which lie beyond the Katmai Pass. They seem too big to be a part of the rest of the world. They do not connect up with the little things which are built into our lives.

D.B. Church, 1917[6]

Dr. Griggs, a botanist by training, carefully noted the beginnings of revegetation in the Valley. As early as 1917 he found algae and mosses — and later, extensive mats of liverworts — thriving "in places bathed by the warm breath of the fumarole."

A later visitor compared Griggs' observations to his own:

In the twenty-odd years since the last expedition of the National Geographic Society, most of the fumaroles had died. With widespread desiccation, algae and mosses had practically vanished from the Valley floor. Warm steam no longer permeated the tuff, which was cold and dry. Rain falling on the tuff ran off at once. The result was the most sterile habitat imaginable.

The extensive mats of liverworts that Griggs found in 1930 had nearly or quite vanished by 1953-54. I found no trace of them in walking many miles, covering the upper portion of the Valley. Grasses, sedges, and other seed plants, however, were present in some abundance, particularly along the bottoms of shallow depressions. In these low places moisture collected during summer rains and as melting snow, but not in such amounts as to rush off immediately. Even here the plants survived only with great difficulty, for surface moisture tended to sink quickly through the very porous ground. Desiccation was a major hazard, and the plants growing on the ash had developed enormous root systems, which also served to anchor the plants against another serious enemy — wind. Numerous willows showed evidence of sand-blasting by the violent williwaws that sweep the Valley in winter.

adapted from Victor Cahalane[7]

Life is coming back, ever so slowly. Even today, the image the Valley presents to the distant viewer is one of utter barrenness.

The vegetation and land forms of Katmai obviously vary with altitude. Along the lakeshores alder, willows, birch, and white spruce are intermingled with stately balsam poplars several feet thick. Fireweed and cotton grass are common; and you find a profusion of berries from delicious highbush cranberries and nagoonberries to poisonous baneberries. As you climb higher, willows predominate; and purple Jacob's ladder and arnica may vie in beauty with white Labrador tea. Still higher is open tundra with blueberries to satisfy bears not gorged with salmon and a myriad of tundra flowers — yellow poppies, Kamchatka rhododendron, roseroot, and alpine azalea.

Ogden Williams[8]

As soon as the salmon begin to enter the streams, bruin makes fishing the chief business. . . . It is most interesting to watch an old she bear with cubs. The cubs do not attempt to fish, but stay on the bank and receive contributions. The old she bear stands upright and wades in water even up to her neck, going very slowly with the current, watching the water and scarcely making a ripple in it. She holds her arms down at her sides with her hands spread, and when she feels a salmon coming up against her, clutches it with her claws and throws it out on the bank to the expectant cubs. Often she stands perfectly motionless for a considerable time, and when she moves, it is with extreme deliberation and caution. After supplying the cubs she puts the next fish in her mouth and goes ashore to eat it. If salmon are plentiful or easily obtained, the two sides of a fish are all that she will eat; sometimes she even scorns these and fastidiously crunches the head and leaves the rest.

Wilfred H. Osgood, 1904

There must have been fifty red salmon inside a miniscule lagoon — most of them bunched closely with snouts above water, the remainder scattered around in varying degrees of weakness, including a pair that had navigated the twenty feet of streambed to the rocks (which was as far as they could go) and were almost imperceptibly moving to stay with the slight current, but so near death they had little movement left in them. Outside the one-foot-deep lagoon, in the lake proper, were another fifty or sixty salmon, milling. Scattered on the sand and across the bottom of the lagoon, some half out of the water, were another forty in varying stages of decay. . . .

As we left two hours later . . . I wanted very much to know why we had been so overwhelmed by what we had seen, feeling absolutely sure that some dead and dying fish were merely the tip of the iceberg.

More than two years later the answer finally came. At a distance of a few feet, that morning at the back of the cove, we had witnessed the explosion of a star. Death scene? Hell, no. Those salmon had been gone five years but they had returned — to pass it along. We had stumbled onto a small yet infinite stage, explosive with the power of lifeforce, manifested there by salmon holding to a genuinely predestined rendezvous — a rendezvous with *life*; and the energy that had driven them for five years and was being passed on was every bit as powerful as the energy that blows the chemistry of a star across the light years.

Dave Bohn[9]

From the Baked Mountain Cabin Log [10]

... Headed for Katmai Crater via Novarupta. Camped at base of Knife Creek Glacier. Got flooded and blown out. Headed back to Baked Mtn. Weathered in for 1 day. Headed back to Knife Creek Glacier for another shot at Katmai Crater. Made it up this time. Saw a most beautiful lake and excellent waterfalls and glaciers running into lake. Clear weather for about 90 minutes. Fog bank moved in so headed down.

Anonymous

This valley is a geologist's heaven — so many geological forces exhibited here in the evolution of the area that it overwhelms me. A great natural laboratory for the pursuit of knowledge. Beautiful sunset too! And the full moon illuminating the valley at night. Does the valley's beauty ever cease to amaze?

Joe

Lovely sunset & early to bed. Woke in the night to view amazing stars, the arc of the aurora borealis & a few shifting curtains. Moonrise late over Mt. Katmai, a rising sliver of light, even in its last phase, brilliant. Next awakening was to the sun rising in the moon's place over the mountain, and the colors of sunset and sunrise are known by all who travel this Valley.

Elizabeth Mills

... The beauty of this place is beyond any words that I can write. It must be experienced — the misery of hiking in the rain, crossing streams while your legs are turning blue, plunging into Mageik lake on an early sunlit morn, the views — oh my gosh one could rant and rave about them for eternity. One day of sun here makes up for all the unpleasantries one can imagine. ...

Katmai may you always remain wild, majestic and intolerable to sissy's.

James Geyer

So the Valley of Ten Thousand Smokes will change, it is not a valley of smokes anymore and one time it will not be very different at all from the other valleys in the monument. What looks like devastation and ruin at first sight, really is creation. In nature nothing is destroyed, things are only changed all the time and no condition is better or worse than it was before.

Aljos Farjon,
Netherlands

... This place is truely hard to believe; the desolation, the elements, the art work on the grandest scale imaginable, are awe inspiring.

Michael Holthus

So clear all day I can't believe this is the same violently windy & notoriously rainy valley I've heard about. Dayhiked today thru Katmai Pass and climbed up to the top of Trident for a no less than spectac. view of Katmai River, Shelikoff Strait & phenomenally clear Kodiak Is. and Naknek Lake as well. Already this trip has been a dream come true. If I can go by the little I know about weather my guess is tomorrow should be as nice. The silence is deafening — we're exhausted after today's hike and climb — Staring over at Mt. Griggs we've decided to give it a climb on our way out of the Valley in about ten days. Looking forward to a day of complete relaxation tomorrow — Sunset is now a rich orange. Clouds look like some of the rocks I've seen. We're alone tonite at the cabin. So wonderfully lonely! God gave us this day!

Anonymous

*The prelude
of hell . . .*

Ancient volcanic outbursts spewed 15 cubic miles of lava and ash to create Aniakchak caldera on the Alaska Peninsula. The colossal eruption blew out or undermined the inner chambers of the volcano, causing its summit to collapse. Later eruptions helped shape the floor of the caldera, creating new lava flows and raising small vents through which the earth spouted more ash and rock.

This older and larger cousin of Katmai is 30 square miles in extent and 6 miles from rim to rim. Remote and hidden by weather, the caldera's modern discovery was delayed until 1922, when a government geologist noticed that higher elevations in the area formed a circle on the map he was making. Members of the U.S. Geological Survey party followed the map's lead and found a huge crater 21 miles in circumferance.

The find intrigued the Jesuit geologist and explorer, Father Bernard Hubbard. His 1930 visit revealed that Aniakchak " . . . encircles with its 3,000-foot walls a variety of scenic features and an abounding bird, animal, fish, and plant life that make it a world in itself — a world inside a mountain."

He got there just in time, for the very next spring Aniakchak erupted again. Violent explosions over many days culminated in a stupendous blast that blew great quantities of rock and ash miles into the sky, where wind transported the ash over vast areas of Alaska and bordering seas.

Father Hubbard hurried to this scene of massive destruction, and with three students began the trek from his base camp at Kujulik Bay to the still-smoking caldera. The priestly scholar's accounts of "Paradise Found," the eruption, and "Paradise Lost" dramatically portray the human problem of keeping up with Alaska's geologic pace.

The caldera floor is the core of Aniakchak. Though quiescent now, it remains an awesome scene of devastation. Its warm springs signal the presence of hot magma just beneath the surface, a hint of future violence. Towering walls isolate and enclose the caldera. Cinder cones rise from its floor. Scattered across it are the charred debris and strange formations of past volcanic discharges. Ancient lava flows spread out from plugged vents in twisted streams of rock. In one corner of the crater, warm springs feed Surprise Lake. The Aniakchak River drains the lake and rushes through a spectacular gash in the caldera's rim on its way to the Pacific Ocean.

Nowhere in North America can nature's sudden, shattering power be better understood than at Aniakchak. The giant shell of the collapsed mountain lies exposed like a geology text opened to the chapter on volcanism. ∎

PARADISE FOUND — *Aniakchak in 1930*

The yellow grass was sending up new shoots of life, the alders were greening, and catkins appeared on the willows. We had to watch our step to keep from treading on the cleverly hidden nests of ptarmigan and grouse that rose continually from almost underneath our feet.

We had expected to find nothing but sterile wastes inside the volcano, and the amount and variety of life astonished us. On the first day we saw, in addition to the game birds just mentioned, numberless smaller birds flying about, eagles soaring overhead, a lone raven squawking raucously, ducks whirring past, and bos'n birds and sea gulls circling over the lake. Ever and anon a bos'n bird would dive into the placid waters to emerge with a shining fingerling in its beak.

The lake, though inside a volcano, was a spawning bed for salmon; and piratical trout fed on the millions of fingerlings. Foxes, which had turned a lava cone near the lake into an apartment house, watched us curiously whenever we approached, yapping at our intrusion.

A trail around the margin of the lake was deeply indented where great brown bears, stepping characteristically in the same tracks for generations, had made holes almost a foot deep. Subsequent findings

showed that bears were always in and around the crater, and that many hibernated in the lava caves.

The fish, game, and bird life was even surpassed by the variety and profusion of flowers, particularly orchids. The more we observed, the more fully were we convinced that Aniakchak was a world complete in itself inside an exploded volcano!

THE ERUPTION — *May 1931*

With all these reports [of volcanic activity] coming from various parts of the great 2,000-mile volcanic rift that forms the Alaska Peninsula and Aleutian Islands, no wonder that I began to look for the climax in a major eruption. It came — and it was Aniakchak.

. . . May 1, 1931, dawned clear and bright on the Alaska Peninsula. Winter had departed from the shore line and the snows had begun to retreat up the lower slopes of the mountains, but winter still maintained its icy grasp on the interior. The trapping season was over and the handful of hardy men who seek a livelihood from the furs of this section were preparing their fishing boats for the summer run on Bering Sea. Among their number was Frank Wilson, one of the few white inhabitants of Meshik. He was scraping and calking his boat when an exclamation of surprise called his attention to his little daughter Mabel playing in the sand near by. She was pointing excitedly at the peak of snow of Aniakchak, fifteen miles away, whence a dense column of white steam was shooting miles high into the sky.

Wilson noted the time. It was ten o'clock a.m. There were none of the preliminary symptoms that are usual with volcanic eruptions. No earthquake shook the ground, nor were any rumbles heard from the nearby mountain. For two hours the white smoke rose in billowing clouds. It was probably steam generated from some fissure in the volcano floor that allowed water to reach the smouldering, buried rocks below. Then, at twelve o'clock, came a terrific explosion. A dense black cloud of incandescent gas and ashes rushed more than 20,000 feet into the air, spread out like a tremendous mushroom and started to descend rapidly. Wilson and his family rushed to their cabin, as did the few fear-stricken Aleuts of Meshik. The earth shook, flame and smoke rose thousands of feet high, and the pyrotechnic display of individual lava bombs hurtling through the air combined with the lightning forming in the cloud to make a truly fear-inspiring sight. Thunder added its din to the almost constant explosions of the erupting volcano, and the sides of the mountain reverberated to the crash of the falling rocks.

PARADISE LOST — *June 1931*

Climbing to the crater rim, we were going through a valley of death in which not a blade of grass or a flower or a bunch of moss broke through the thick covering of deposited ash. Black cinders clinked under our feet and slid away. . . . Several hours of hard work, and but a few feet separated us from the coveted goal, the rim of Aniakchak, and the first glance into the great abyss. . . . Kneeling, as is our custom on such occasions, we said our "Hail Mary" aloud; then crawled cautiously to the edge. Silence. Nobody wanted to speak. There was the new Aniakchak, but it was the abomination of desolation, it was the prelude of hell. Black walls, black floor, black water, deep black holes and black vents; it fairly agonized the eye to look at it. No longer did the beautifully colored lavas and shiny volcanic glass strike the vision. No streams coursed through flower-strewn meadows, no grassy slopes led up to former volcanic vents; no glistening glaciers or snowfields broke the monotony of the huge crater walls. No contorted lava flows pleased with the sinuous windings of their cooling masses. . . . Vent Mountain, rising in the center of the great crater, had an ominous crack in its side and its top was covered with clouds and gas. Beautiful Surprise Lake, nestled under the northern rim, was choked, and muddy and black were its shores, and filled its coves.

And the cause of it all? Far off under the opposite

rim to us, more than six and a half miles away, a new sight greeted our eyes. There was a huge black crater built out from the wall, and from its black maw yellow and brown gases were pouring, and clouds of escaping steam. A few miles to the left of this new main vent a lava hill was being pushed up above the crater floor, its top a mass of cracking, tumbling blocks the size of houses, and from every crack streams of gas and steam were issuing. Beyond the moving hill a seemingly bottomless pit had been blown out of the crater floor, and smoke was pouring from it too. But the terrible blackness of it all got on our nerves. Visibility was none too good, as it had not rained for a few days and dust whirlwinds danced along the crater floor like some mad ghosts that danced their devil's ball in the deadly smoke and gases of this vision of hell in Aniakchak.

The Aniakchak River, in a series of white rapids, tumbled out of the crater. Its waters were heavy with suspended ashes, and the canyon walls that rose 1,000 feet above were sliding with ashes that tried to cling to every ledge. Roping for safety, we climbed along the river's edge until we arrived at the crater floor. Here the desolation of Paradise Lost was even more impressive than when seen from the rim.

Where streams that teemed with spawning salmon had wound to Surprise Lake, where flower-strewn meadows had smiled, where birds and beasts had found food and sanctuary, and pleasant coves along the lake had made inviting camp sites — now all was blotted out in one mighty cataclysm.

. . . A few hours of hard walking over sliding ashes and we neared the first explosion pit, blown out of the crater floor just under the southwestern wall of the crater. Puffs of smoke and clouds of steam were billowing out of what appeared to be a bottomless pit. The gases grew stronger and the ground hotter as we gingerly approached its edge. And then it opened up with a suddenness that made us dizzy.

Color was the first impression. We had been going through only gray and black for days, until we wondered if there was any color left in the world. Here it was, a huge paint pot. Yellow sulphurs seethed and boiled around the edge of broken blocks of red lava that filled the pit. Colored fumes too heavy to rise rolled about like waves on a stormy sea. Now and then came a crackle as one portion grew hotter than the rest and began to flow. The pit itself was the smallest of the several holes blown out of the crater floor, though it was more than a mile in circumference.

We approached the huge built-up crater where the main explosion had taken place. Long before we reached it, the crater floor showed evidence of the terrible eruption. Huge bulges and open cracks appeared. Loose ashes changed to heavy cinders, and grotesque bombs of volcanic origin of every shape and size lined the floor. They had been blown miles high, and descending, had hit with such tremendous force that each bomb had scooped out a craterlet, bouncing off and making smaller holes until it came to a stop. . . .

Climbing the sloping sides of the new subcrater was arduous, as nothing was solid. The skin was almost scraped from our hands and fingernails were lacerated, while our faces and hair were scorched with heat and gas. We could not rest content until we saw the main effect of the cataclysm, so up we struggled until we gained the steaming rim. A look into the crater maw was terrifying. Black, ash-covered lava moved uneasily in the center of a three-mile-circumference hole. Around its edge sulphur boiled in a sea like so much porridge. It came out as a heavy gas and deposited its scintillating yellow masses in solid form against the crater walls, only to become top-heavy, and fall in blocks, a ton or more in weight, back into the boiling mass, to seethe awhile and re-form again. A bluish haze indicative of extremely high temperatures came from the pit, and invisible gases condensed high above the heated mass.

We stood awestricken on the edge, looking, like Dantes, into a real inferno.

Bernard Hubbard[1]

*Showplace
of the earth . . .*

From a mile-high icefield on the Kenai Peninsula, glaciers tumble in crevassed cascade to fjords below. These flooded valleys, carved by glaciers of an earlier epoch, extend seaward into the Gulf of Alaska. Peninsulas separating the fjords are the partly submerged remnants of mountains and ridges, their ice-scalloped alpine topography now prey to pounding surf.

At the height of the Ice Age, a continuous ice cap thousands of feet deep covered the entire Kenai-Chugach mountain chain. Only the highest peaks protruded above the white expanse. Harding Icefield preserves a relict segment of that ancient landscape.

This incredible scenery results from an astounding combination of natural forces. Displacements caused by the collision of tectonic plates both build mountains and drag them under. The jamming impact of the expanding Pacific Plate crumples up the margin of the North American continent. Then, as the Pacific Plate slides under, it drags the leading edge of the North American Plate down with it.

The mountains produced by tectonic uplift trap moisture blowing off the Gulf of Alaska, whose storms dump about 400 inches of snow each year onto Harding Icefield. Pushed outward by the pressures of accumulating snow, the flowing tendrils of the icefield sculpt the mountains to alpine delicacy and perfection.

Then the edge of the glaciated coastline subsides into the sea. There are records of catastrophic subsidence during the earthquakes that register movements of tectonic plates — landscapes sinking 40 or 50 feet at a time. In the great Alaska earthquake of 1964, this coast slid another 7 feet into the sea. This explains how a glacial cirque, carved by ice on a mountaintop, can now be a bay in a peninsula of Kenai Fjords.

Outriders of the peninsulas — islands, sea stacks, and sentinel rocks — are part of the Alaska Maritime National Wildlife Refuge. Thousands of seabirds breed on these isolated flecks of land. Wanderers of distant oceans, many of these birds come to shore only for breeding. Fractured rocks on the margins of the wave-battered islands make convenient hauling-out ledges for sea lions.

Sea otters frequent clear shallow waters along the rocky coast. But harbor seals, able to hunt in turbid water, prefer the inner fjords near glacial fronts, where ice floes provide resting places and refuges for their pups.

Uniting the mile-high icefield with the sea are the tidewater glaciers and the multitudes of roaring cascades and torrent streams that descend from hanging glaciers trapped in high valleys. Close to the waterline, a fringing forest of spruce and hemlock shelters forest predators — black bear, marten, and fox. Scrambling above them, mountain goats forage the rocky slopes and steeps.

The delicate yet rugged beauty of Kenai Fjords is the product of massive geologic forces and erosive waters — solid and liquid, fresh and salt. Life teems along the shoreline oasis and in the bordering sea. But the icefield is a lofty, glistening desert, a crystallized world of unsullied beauty. ∎

The Alaska coast is to become the showplace of the earth, and pilgrims, not only from the United States, but from far beyond the seas, will throng in endless processions to see it.

Henry Gannett, 1899

With kayaks strapped on the boat's aft deck . . . we motored out of Seward. An hour and a half later we rounded Aialik Cape. Vertical cliffs dropped to the water. Islands and rocks were pounded by the waves. In bad weather and heavy seas the cape is extremely treacherous. Currents suck the water about, and reverberations of waves from the rock make the passage awash with chop. A bald eagle posed high on a

towering rock.

The seas smoothed quickly. Chat Island passed on the left, and to the right Chat Cove lay still and quiet. . . . All the shores remained rock or cliff bound.

We motored into Bear Cove and spied a beach and campsite at about the cove's center. Very little surge touched the steep rock beach. We unloaded the kayaks, eager to put in at last.

We paddled next to the shore . . . . A sea otter was startled by us, slipped into the water, and swam under us in his escape. Water from the snow-capped heights cascaded into the cove. Several kinds of jellyfish pulsated through the water. A seal curiously watched us, keeping his distance.

We watched the weather closely, as we knew that winds can kick up rapidly in the fjords, and that even in the protected bays and coves, seas can quickly build. As the afternoon passed dark clouds appeared over the ridges above us. A wind began to blow so we paddled back to camp.

No luck fishing, so dehydrated dinner was prepared. We made a fire, using driftwood and the branches of dead trees. A light rain began as we ate dinner, and continued through the night.

Charles Gilbert

Notice to Hunters
DUE TO THE FACT OF BAD
WEATHER - EITHER IN SEWARD
OR WHERE YOUR CAMP IS - BE
PREPARED AND FORWARNED.
YOU MAY BE WEATHERED IN UP
TO A WEEK OR MORE PAST YOUR
PICK-UP DAY. IN THIS CASE -
DUE TO PRIORITY - THOSE WHO HA
BEEN WEATHERED IN THE LONGEST
ARE FIRST IN LINE FOR PICK-UP.
AS WEATHER PERMITS. PLEASE
BREAK CAMP WITHOUT DELAY WHEN
THE PLANE COMES - FOR WE HAVE
OTHERS ALSO WAITING FOR PICK-UP.
WE WILL PICK YOU UP AS SOON
AS ITS SAFE TO FLY.
PRIORITY FIRST

Posted in a bush pilot's office in Seward, this caution speaks volumes — not only about preparations for physical survival, but also about the serenity of resignation. Alaska is a place where weather and isolation can combine suddenly to frustrate human control of events. No phone, no taxi, no emergency service . . . no recourse but to hunker in and wait. Such times can be terribly upsetting to people long tyrannized by calendars and schedules. On the other hand — assuming that physical needs are met — such times can be pleasant, indeed, particularly in the settings where these adventures are likely to occur.

The victim of Nature's caprice, having lost control,

can relax. It's free time. It can be a window on the timelessness that goes on around us, all the time.

Paradise Cove, Beauty Bay, Beautiful Island, Surprise Bay, and Delight Lake. These names reflected the impressions made on early explorers by the inside waters of Alaska's Kenai Fjords. Their impressions of the outer coast sang another song: Wildcat Pass, Thunder Bay, Cloudy Cape, and Roaring Cove.

M. Woodbridge Williams

If the day is clear, you can look above the sheer ice cliffs and up the glacial valley to distant cornices almost a mile above your boat, up where the great rim of the Harding Icefield brims over its montane platform. . . .

The Katmai eruption of 1912 spewed volcanic ash over much of the Kenai Peninsula, and some of that ash is now being exposed in glaciers flowing down from the main icefield. From this, it can be deduced that the glacial ice has a cycle of about seventy years. Yet, the glacier seems as old as time. Strange, too, how a glacier catches the eye even at a great distance. It is always the center of attention in its particular landscape, as you might expect any huge living thing to be. . . .

Another roar as a mass of ice calved into the sea. The sound, rather than the size of the icefall, gave some perspective of the glacier's dimension. An insignificant dribble of ice had flaked away from the glacial face, pouring down in slow motion, and then a stentorian rumble reached us and we could see a ground swell rising and coming on.

John Madson[1]

The endless icefield, like the desert, completely fooled our sense of distance.

J. Vin Hoeman

We spent our first morning crossing the Resurrection River. The stream was high from melting snow and too deep and swift to wade. Jim swam across and we set up a Tyrolean traverse, hauling the packs, skis, and food across the river on ropes. The rest of us, being too heavy for the elastic nylon ropes, then swam

the ice-cold stream. . . . there was a certain finality in crossing the river; a physical and symbolic separation from the road on the other side.

The rest of the day was spent ferrying loads to the base of Exit Glacier. During the next three days we climbed up to the icefield: first climbing with crampons

on the bare ice of the glacier's snout, then back onto the land to bypass a dangerously crevassed area. Our fourth night was spent on the last outcrop of rock and tundra at the edge of the icefield. . . . The view is outstanding. Down to the left is Exit Glacier, a heavily crevassed and contorted tongue of ice cutting a steep canyon down to Resurrection Valley. It contrasts sharply with Harding Icefield which stretches out to the southwest, a smooth sea of snow with only a few nunataks rising above it.

The next day was cloudy but still clear enough to travel out onto the icefield. Carrying heavy packs and dragging two sleds, we headed for a nunatak ten miles to the southwest. After a few hours the cloud ceiling dropped and a furious storm started, forcing us to camp. For a day and a half we waited for the storm to let up — cooking, eating, sleeping and trying to stay dry as the wet snow drifted against our tents. After forty hours of continuous snow and wind, the storm eased up and the visibility improved. By the time we broke camp the sky was blue. We quickly pushed on into the center of the icefield. For three days we travelled as much as we could, only sleeping five or six hours each night. We wanted to cross the icefield before another storm caught and held us.

We descended the Tustumena Glacier until it became heavily crevassed and then left it for solid ground on the south side. After five days on glacial ice and snow, the rock and sparse vegetation seemed luxurious. Now we could travel unroped and without skis, and we could drink water without first melting snow. The sterility of the icefield made us appreciate that which we had hardly noticed before.

Bill Resor

The first Fork-tailed Storm Petrel of the study was discovered on Outer Island in the Pye Island group. Outer Island is the first location we had encountered where habitat is suitable for petrels and where predators have not been introduced. Its exposed

position places it in the midst of the currents of the
Gulf of Alaska and the tidal currents of the Kenai Fjords.
Rich feeding grounds therefore lie just off the island.

On Matushka Island we counted the Rhino Auklet
burrows and came up with a total of 180. They were in
a forested part of the island, dug in a peaty soil under
the tree roots. The ground around the burrows had
been tramped down, and supported no vegetation. Care
had to be taken in walking through the colony as our
weight could crush some of the burrows. On the south
and east sides of Matushka Island there are very large
numbers of murres, kittiwakes, gulls, and puffins.
Matushka Island took on great charm for us. It was the
most interesting island we visited, boasting an amazing
variety of species and abundance of sea birds.

Charles Gilbert
notes from a seabird survey, 1976

Alaska's epitome . . .

Distilled in the Lake Clark country are the many splendors of Alaska. In this one place — compressed and crafted by Nature's several forces — classic natural landscapes crowd together: fjords, coastal rain forest, glaciated mountains overtopped by ragged peaks and steaming volcanoes, pendant mountain lakes, and river-laced foothills fading into tundra plains and boreal forest.

Backdropping a coast partly rugged, partly alluvial, mountain chains come together in echelon — the Alaska Range to the north, then the Chigmit Mountains, and the Aleutian Range to the south. Surface drainages and passes mark their jointings and the underlying faults where tectonic powers bide their time.

Glaciers drape this perplexity of mountains. Streams pour from hanging glaciers, veiling cliffsides as they fall to wild rivers far below. Through labyrinthian canyons carved by Ice Age glaciers, the rivers flow to basins dammed by the moraines of those ancient glaciers. Thus has ice ploughed and water filled the land to create the string of lovely lakes adorning the west flank of the mountains.

Unlike the open Arctic or the giant Wrangell Mountains, the Lake Clark country is tight and intricate and comprehendable. It is filled with pocket valleys, narrow canyons, and cameo meadows. These are bounded by massive mountain walls, which themselves are broken by the cirques, hanging valleys, and winding passes produced by vigorous glacial erosion. The effect of these alternating enclosures and openings is first to focus the eye on near scenes of exquisite alpine beauty, then to draw the view to slotted vistas of distant scarps, waterfalls, and far mountains. It is an esthetic combination of near unity and distant mystery.

Landscape diversity is matched by varied plant and animal life in the transitions from marine to mountain to lowland habitats. The region straddles the margins of many life zones — Sitka spruce grow no farther north, Dall sheep and black bear range no farther south and southwest.

Lake Clark, extending far into the mountains, gathers the ultimate sources of the Kvichak River system, the world's richest spawning and rearing waters for red salmon. A major purpose of the parkland is to help protect the watershed necessary for perpetuation of the red salmon. Both local subsisters and the important Bristol Bay commercial fishery depend on the health of this ecosystem. Brown bear inhabit the parkland's lower elevations. During salmon runs they concentrate along the major spawning streams fringing the lakes. Black bear favor dense timber stands along the lake shores.

The tundra plain on the west margin of the area supports a range of tundra types from dry to moist, providing varied habitat for caribou, moose, and birds. Two of its several drainages, the Mulchatna and the Chilakadrotna, have been designated wild rivers. They flow from Turquoise Lake and Twin Lakes, respectively, then skirt caribou calving grounds in the Bonanza Hills. The Tlikakila, also a wild river, rises in Lake Clark Pass and traverses 50 miles of spectacular mountain scenery before braiding into the upper end of Lake Clark.

The marine coastal environment provides choice habitat for many of Lake Clark's predatory birds, including bald eagle and osprey. Razor clams and other shoreline invertebrates help sustain the large fish, beluga whales, seals, and sea- and shorebirds that frequent this part of the parkland.

Lake Clark is not Alaska's biggest, highest, or most remote wilderness. But its diverse physiography comprehends what is probably the most complete microcosm of Alaska's scenic, wildlife, and geologic resources. Sheltered by its mountain ramparts, it was, until the advent of the floatplane, one of the state's most isolated fastnesses. Even today, away from the lake shores, there is hardly any evidence of human presence. The historic trails of Native traders between Bristol Bay and Cook Inlet are overgrown, except where maintained by wandering animals. ∎

Something of most parts of Alaska is represented here, but more tersely. The Brooks Range and other Alaskan wilderness areas are elaborate novels; this is a poem.

Bob Waldrop[1]

Our first view of Lake Clark . . . was not an impressive one, as we were so situated that only the lower end, where the shores are comparatively low, could be seen. When once on the lake itself, however, with an unobstructed vista of the greater part of its length, the view was magnificent. The mountains . . . extend along each side of the narrow stretch of water, and gradually become higher and higher and more and more rugged. . . . Those about the upper end are steep and but slightly eroded, being too precipitous in most places to hold large snow banks. On the south side near the upper end, however, several small, high-hanging glaciers may be seen at the head of narrow canyons.

Wilfred H. Osgood, 1904

The Chigmits form the meeting place of the massive Alaska and Aleutian ranges that dominate the state's southern half, and it is as if colliding mountain waves have thrown up a storm of rock. To some, they are Alaska's Alps, so tight and deep a mountain maze that each portion is a private world. Only the doughtiest trekkers have crossed the Chigmits on foot, braving flood and thicket and crevasse.

Think of all the splendors that bespeak Alaska: glaciers, volcanoes, alpine spires, wild rivers, lakes with grayling on the rise. Picture coasts feathered with countless seabirds. Imagine dense forests and far-sweeping tundra, herds of caribou, great roving bears. Now concentrate all these and more into less than one percent of the state — and behold the Lake Clark region, Alaska's epitome.

John Kauffmann[2]

Telaquana Lake is used as a resting area for thousands of waterfowl during their fall migration south. They migrate through the canyon at the east end of the lake and apparently through the Neacola River canyon to the eastern side of the Alaska Range. When the canyon at the east end of Telaquana Lake is blocked by fog or during a snow storm, I have seen the east end of the lake literally fill up with thousands of ducks, geese, and swans. When the canyon clears, the waterfowl depart within a few hours. None of the other lakes, except perhaps Lake Clark and Two Lakes, receive such waterfowl populations.

Richard R. Straty

Here on Lake Clark we seem to be more aware of the progression of the year and of the seasons and the weather than ever before. Perhaps it is because our comings and goings are so dependent on the weather and the wind and the hours of daylight. . . . Our front window faces east and south and we mark the progress of the year by the place the sun chooses to peak from behind the mountains each morning. Now, during the dark months, we sit before the window and drink our morning coffee and watch for the sun each day. Each morning the sunrise is different, but beautiful and special. Some mornings there are cloud layers that diffuse and reflect the sun's rays in many glorious combinations of colors. Once in a great while when we have a heavy overcast, the sun will find one hole and beam through like a giant searchlight. On clear mornings, the mountains stand in magnificent silhouette gradually revealing all their details as the sun rises higher in the sky. The mountains themselves put on a different face for each season. In the winter when they are completely covered with snow they are a lesson in geometry, all lines and angles and planes. When some of the snow melts or blows off they begin to look like a masterpiece in pen and ink with the black lines of spruce and rocky ridges against the white of the snow. Spring with wildflowers and new leaves, summer with full dark leaves and berries, and autumn with gold of birch and cottonwood and scarlet and purple of blueberry and bearberry covers the sharp edges, softens the lines and the mountains are less forbidding and rugged, more accessible. In the evenings once in a great while they will glow red in the sunset — Lake Clark Alpenglow. Although we can enjoy the colors of the sunset in the evening sky from home, to see the full sunset we must climb the cliff and that we often do for it is a sight well worth seeing — the earth turning from the sun for another day, the beautiful colors shining out over the Chulitna river. . . .

Soon the seed catalogs will come and we will send off our orders. By March the house will be full of baby plants and in April we will start the greenhouse and move the plants down there. The swans and ducks, eagles, hawks, songbirds will return. Alaska is a beautiful place to live and we appreciate the good fortune that made it possible for us to live here especially on Lake Clark.

Sara and Chuck Hornberger

The [parkland] lies just west of Cook Inlet. *Stormbird*, a 65-foot former Army boat, refitted and skippered by charter captain Clem Tillion, took me there through the inlet's choppy swells. . . . At magnificent Tuxedni Bay, two gateposts tower nearly two miles high. Backlighted and pale with snow, they seem at first immutably frozen, yet steam seeps from the side of one. They are active volcanoes: Iliamna and Redoubt.

Other, lesser mountain steeps join them, walling off the Tuxedni coast with an awesome fortress that grew steadily more imposing during our sea-level approach. White cataracts spumed down furrowed cliffs hundreds of feet high.

"This is the beginning of the country I really like," Clem said. "It's clear and clean and absolutely wild. Like looking at the world as it used to be." Before us, beluga whales sounded in the icy waters of Tuxedni Bay.

Double-crested cormorants wheeled above the high rock prow of Chisik Island, refuge for tens of thousands of seabirds. Sea life of 150 million years ago — ammonites and mussels now preserved in stone — showed in the crumbling, layered cliffs of Fossil Point.

As in the Arctic, summers here are prolific and short, though not as brief as farther north. Tuxedni Bay's sloping ramparts come to life while you watch, growing so alder-green that, through narrowed eyes forgetful of latitude, they seem to form an almost Caribbean coast.

John Kauffmann[3]

Is it proper that the wilderness and its creatures should suffer because we came?

Richard Proenneke[4]

May 21st. I looked around at the wind-blasted peaks and the swirls of mist moving past them. It was hard to take my eyes away. I had been up on some of them, and I would be up there again. There was something different to see each time, and something different from each one. All those streamlets to explore and all those tracks to follow through the glare of the high basins and over the saddles. Where did they lead, what was beyond? What stories were written in the snow?

May 23rd. When the fog finally cleared the face of the mountain across the ice, I sighted a bunch of eleven Dall ewes and lambs. Five lambs in all, a good sign. A mountain has got to be lonely without sheep on it.

June 15th. A beautiful evening with a light breeze down the lake. A loon rode low in the water and trailed a wake of silver as it took flight.

July 2nd. Rags of fog now. The wisps blown on a damp wind from out of the snow fields, curling, spreading, disappearing. Finally, there it was, my observatory among the black boulders; two hours from the lowlands. No wonder the eagle soars the high places. Far below was the valley of Emerson Creek, with its many waterfalls in feeder streams that tumbled their courses from the snow saddle in the mists. Peaks all around me, some granite-ribbed and snow-blotched, some stabbing up starkly on either side of the glacier that curved between them like a great white, blue-rutted highway. Others were off in the direction of the lower lake, huge mounds of marble cake streaked in green shadows, all with a regal bearing that awed a man in their presence.

I watched the ravens rising and floating and falling in and out of the mist above the crags that reared from the great snow field. Their whoops and guttural yelps sounded as though they were coming over an amplifier in the vast stillness. They have a lot to talk about. . . .

Clouds piled on the tops of some far peaks. A man could get lost in himself up there. I munched on my biscuit sandwiches, my eyes following the flight of an eagle below. His white head and tail caught the sun as he searched beneath him. Sailing and circling, the wind currents lifting, gently buffeting him as he soared.

Everywhere I looked was fascination. Those great masses of broken rock that the mountain sheep bounced over as lightly as if on level ground. Chunks of the peaks falling away over the years had made these treacherous accumulations, like enormous tailing piles of giant prospectors.

Gleaming snowfields showed not a sign of a track. They would be blinding to walk across in the bright sun. And all those beautiful waterfalls, some dropping from the high buttresses like thin streams of molten silver and seeming to vanish in midair. Others along the creek below spilled in wide bright aprons between banks as green as new leaves.

To see game you must move a little and look a lot. What first appears to be a branch turns into that big caribou bull up there on the benches. . . . I wonder what he thinks about? . . . I wonder if he feels as I do, that this small part of the world is enough to think about?

Richard Proenneke[5]

*The sense
of the great
mountains . . .*

The Wrangell-Saint Elias region contains the most extensive realm of mountains, icefields, and glaciers in North America. Together with neighboring Kluane National Park in Canada, it has been designated a World Heritage Area by the United Nations. Its awesome magnificence compares to the Himalayas, the Andes, and the frozen cordilleras of Antarctica. The scale of its grandeur, the bold strokes that shaped the land, beggar description and guard the kingdom.

At this curve of the continent the concentric arcs of the Pacific mountain system bend together in a sweeping westerly turn. The volcanic massif of the Wrangell Mountains acts as pivot for this vast rotation. South of the Wrangells, across the forested valley of the Chitina River, the Chugach Mountains rise above broad glaciers bordering the sea. East of the Wrangells, across the gash of Chitistone Canyon, the rugged Saint Elias Range soars toward the finlike peak of Mount Saint Elias, more than 18,000 feet above sea level. North of the Wrangells the foothills blend into the Alaska Range, which arches toward the distant heights of Mount McKinley.

Perhaps a third of this largest of all United States parklands is covered with perpetual ice and snow. There are great expanses of bare rock — scarps and sidewalls — and many long ridges and high benches that would be major mountains in other settings. Rivers flow in all directions from the clustered masses of mountains. They are wild glacial streams, snaking out of moraines and carving canyons through brilliantly colored formations or fractured walls of dark lava: Nizina, Bremner, White, Chisana, Nabesna. The Copper, one of Alaska's major rivers, heads on the north side of 16,200-foot Mount Sanford then curves south to the gulf, forming the parkland's western boundary. Its largest tributary, the west-flowing Chitina, taps icefields and glaciers that straddle the international boundary. Its network of side canyons and valleys probes deeply the rimming ranges dominated by 16,400-foot Mount Blackburn, highest of

the Wrangells.

Indeed, the mountains and their associated icefields and glaciers dominate everything in sight from all perspectives. Even when clouds cloak the higher elevations, the massive stumps of the mountains dwarf the lower landscapes and intimidate the imagination that would try to picture those misty heights.

People have tried to quantify this immensity. The parkland contains nine peaks more than 14,000 feet high, four of them rising more than 16,000 feet. There are uncounted peaks in the 10,000- to 14,000-foot range. Storms annually precipitate as much as 50 feet of snow in the upper reaches of the Saint Elias chain and along the Bagley Icefield. The compacting loads of snow feed 75 named glaciers and as many unnamed. The Bering and Nabesna are among the world's longest glaciers. The Malaspina is one of the world's largest piedmont or lowland glaciers. The glaciers, in turn, generate the two dozen river systems that drain the parkland.

These computations do more than simply state bigness. They give insight into a corner of the world so extreme in its physiographic dimensions that it magnifies the effects of natural processes. Again, plate tectonics is the causal root of these colossal mechanics. It uplifts ancient sediments, and it triggers volcanic mountain building. The mountains snare moist winds that mediate between ocean and land. The hydrologic cycle then reverses direction as ice and water obey gravity's pull. Their erosive power chisels the land and carries debris toward the sea. These scoops and gouges produce isolated valleys and outwash plains lost in the general immensity. In these hidden places, blocked by the mountain ramparts from outer disruption, entire ecosystems pursue their destinies.

In the main, human beings have looked with wonder upon this mountain kingdom from a distance. A few have followed its rivers into the walled recesses — hunting, mining, seeking the isolation and peace of those hidden places. A few more have climbed the peaks and traversed the pristine glory of its high icefields.

But most stop at the periphery or in the valley vestibules where the ascending corridors begin to close. This, too, is adventure. From the sea, from the air, from the roads that nearly encircle and in a few places tentatively enter the forelands of Wrangell-Saint Elias, this Valhalla-like place presents a breathtaking beauty. In its very impregnability — guarding all those lost valleys and distant shores where animals roam and birds sing unmolested — there is adventure for the soul. ■

No buoyancy of spirit characterized the party as it left the mouth of the Tazlina, entirely in ignorance of what was in store for it; and, wearied with hunger and other hardships, there was just cause for melancholy. The party had scarcely been dry day or night since leaving Taral [at the mouth of the Chitina River]. During the day we had an accident which might easily have proved fatal to the success of the expedition. In crossing the river, an undertaking circumstances frequently necessitated, our skin boat struck and lodged in the middle of the channel, where the current was terrific, on a huge hidden boulder. The dogs were thrown out of the boat, the sides of which were crushed in, and for a few minutes general consternation prevailed until we were again safe on land. Had the boat upset, our bedding, guns, and instruments would have been lost, and doubtless the lives of some of the party. This event seemed to add no little to the general depression of the party.

Lt. Henry T. Allen, 1885

I. C. Russell, leader of an expedition attempting to climb Mount St. Elias in 1891, gained a divide on the crest of the range at an altitude of 14,500 feet, and from that vantage point viewed for the first time the then unknown area to the north. Russell's impression of the scene is an eloquent description of the St. Elias Mountains:

I expected to see a comparatively low, forested country, stretching away to the north, with lakes and rivers and perhaps some signs of human habitation. What met my astonished gaze was a vast snow-covered region, limitless in expanse, through which hundreds, perhaps thousands, of bare, angular mountain peaks projected. There was not a stream, not a lake, and not a vestige of vegetation of any kind in sight. A more desolate or utterly lifeless land one never beheld. Vast, smooth snow surfaces without crevasses stretched away to limitless distances, broken only by jagged and angular mountain peaks.
So the St. Elias Mountains remain today — desolate, icebound, uninhabited except for a few small settlements around the fringe — still a challenge to the explorer and mountaineer, a vast field laboratory for the student of glaciers.

Don J. Miller[1]

The St. Elias Mountains are the tallest coastal mountains in the world and in terms of slope present greater relief than the Himalayas.

Arctic Institute of North America

The lowland areas of Wrangell-St. Elias can be divided into three distinct zones: To the north, the rain-shadow effect of the Wrangell Mountains produces a relatively dry Interior climate of open country. Several deep, clear, cold-water lakes are set in the rolling tundra and wooded hills of this zone. The central zone comprises the wetter, more heavily vegetated Chitina Valley, laced by many tributary glacial rivers. At its upper end is Chitistone Canyon, combining elements of Grand Canyon and Yosemite in one place. Towering walls a mile high display the geologic history of the region, while the Chitistone River at its bottom continues to actively alter landforms. Finally, the forelands of the Malaspina Glacier and Icy and Yakutat bays include more than 80 miles of coastline, where

broad, level beaches show the power of ferocious storms off the Gulf of Alaska. Behind the sand dunes is a strip of forests intermingled with ponds and bogs. The forests, growing on moraines and in soils overlaying inactive ice of Malaspina Glacier, could be destroyed at any time by a surge of the glacier. The glaciers that calve into Icy and Yakutat bays are among the largest and most active in North America.

Gerald Wright

Near the sources of the Chitina River looms a mammoth glacier that takes its name from a pioneer Alaskan explorer, Robert Kennicott. Overlooking the glacier stand a mill town and mines that made a misspelled variant of his name synonymous with copper wealth throughout the world.

Discovery of the Kennecott mines exposed an ore body unequalled in the 20th Century for its concentrated copper, copper so pure that it had been fashioned into ornaments and trade items by the Athapascan Indians of the region. In these volcanic mountains, heated water had moved bits of copper from igneous rock and deposited them in limestone faults and cracks. Then Ice Age cold had preserved these deposits from dissolution and oxidation. Compared to the 2 percent ores in the American Southwest, Kennecott's first assays of 76 percent pure copper in Chalcocite ores staggered the copper industry, which acclaimed the deposits "the richest outcrops ever discovered."

Evolution of Kennecott from a prospect in 1900 to a center of advanced mining technology and a springboard of corporate power hinged on completion of the Copper River and Northwestern Railroad, which in 1911 replaced horse-drawn sledges as the link between the mines and ocean transportation. Exhaustion of high-grade ores forced Kennecott's close in 1938. But during its three decades of highly profitable production it was a major force in Alaska's history and economy — a smaller scale Prudhoe Bay of its day.

The quick profits made possible by a geologic happenstance fueled financial and corporate enterprises of national and international scope. The well organized company town of Kennecott and its less restrictive neighbor, McCarthy, served the spectrum of human needs. Today these communities go their own ways amidst architectural remains that recall the industrial heydey.

adapted from Melody Webb[2]

The alpine and sub-alpine zones of the Wrangell Mountains contain some 3 million acres of excellent Dall sheep habitat. Perhaps 10,000 sheep live in these favored zones. As a result, the Wrangells long have been Alaska's most important sport hunting area for sheep. The Alaska Lands Act of 1980 recognized this historic use by designating part of the parkland a National Park, where sport hunting is prohibited, and part a National Preserve, where sport hunting is allowed under the constraints of State and Federal law and the principles of scientific wildlife management. Sheep habitat is about equally divided between these designations, thus assuring a large unhunted sanctuary for the sheep. (This same principle applies in a number of the new parklands, where the preserve designation provides basic habitat protection but allows continuation of selected historic uses.)

Sport hunting in national parklands, whatever their designation, is a controversial subject and doubtless will continue to be so. A positive perspective, conditioned by the rules of fair chase and enlightened guiding, is offered in excerpts from a 1974 report by wilderness preservationist John Kauffmann:

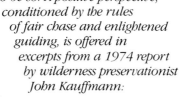

On a ten-day guided fair-chase hunt for Dall sheep I confirmed by personal experience my conviction that this form of recreation is a valid wilderness experience appropriate to certain of the larger park proposals for Alaska. The hunting camp was located on an unnamed lake high in mountainous country that constitutes, in my opinion, the quintessence of wilderness. I shot a good ram after a stalk typical of the sport, on the sixth day after an accumulated 60 miles of hiking.

My guide's three-tent camp with meat rack and two storage barrels was a model of immaculate simplicity; comfortable but with no frills. He had done nothing that was not easily reversible to complete wilderness conditions. Moreover, his sense of stewardship of the game and fish and scenery was commendable in highest terms. For example, although the lake teemed with fish, he allowed but one meal from the lake during the hunt.

I had never hunted big game before, and I enjoyed it. It is a legitimate quest, and I believe many people need such a special incentive and objective to stimulate them to and through a wilderness experience. The hunt brought me very close to the land and its many subtle elements, and I felt a kinship to ages of men and beasts for whom hunting has been a means of survival, a way of life and a meaningful ritual. Like fishing and tilling, climbing and sailing, the hunt was, in a way, a celebration of man's relationship to earth and with all living things.

In a fair-chase hunt that requires time, work, and a certain blending with the environment, the total experience is what counts, not merely the accomplishment of the kill. That is only the climax of a deepening relationship of the hunter toward his environment. In the other kind of hunting, the quick get-a-trophy kind, the hunter deprives himself of that relationship and the insights it provides.

The immensity of geologic features, the diversity of ecological systems, and the grandeur of isolated vastness combine to make the Wrangell Mountain Region a wilderness and scenic resource of international significance. Clearly revealed on the land are the natural processes of volcanism, mountain uplift and glacial action. On this landscape, a range of biologic environments is evolving in response to changing conditions and the advance and retreat of glaciers. Coastal rain forest, taiga, tundra, rivers, lakes and coastal beaches all have a complement of species adapting to an environment of extremes. Immense quantities of water and ice, sediment and geomorphic energy flow through this environment each year, dwarfing the amounts which cycle through milder climates. Living organisms can wrest only a small fraction of this vital flow as they survive under severe conditions. These are the conditions that prevailed over most of North America before the most recent geologic times. The Wrangell Mountain Region, as nowhere else, retains the features and processes which typified the Pleistocene, the time of the ice ages, on the North American continent.

The Wrangell Mountain Project[3]

From the seacoast, the region can be roughly defined at opposite ends by the deep, wide canyons of two enormous glacial rivers, the Copper and the Alsek, which are still carving lonely corridors for waters and wildlife through the otherwise unforgiving expanses.... It is these great glacial torrents, and the still building mountains from which they fall, which provide unity to this largely austere region. While expanses of lowlands, in places flat and marshy, blanket the outwash beyond the slopes, yet the sense of the great mountains always lingers.

Rich Gordon

Because the rivers are derived from glacial melt-water, a stream that might be small and easily fordable in the morning may become a raging torrent by noon of a hot day.

Gerald Wright

Natural processes, both ecological and geological, are striking. The landscape is new and in tumult, primarily under the influence of moving ice. The Russell Glacier has surged and changed in the past few years. On bluffs along the floodplain of the upper White River, recent erosion reveals melting permafrost lenses. These same bluffs contain many feet of peat, interlayered with river sediments and volcanic dust. Stumps from a dozen generations of spruce forest lie exposed in the peat, with the present generation growing from the top layer.

Rich Gordon and Ben Shaine

Anthus spinoletta. Water pipit. Frequent at high elevations throughout the area, on both low-angle tundra slopes and high-angle rocky peaks barren of vegetation. These birds are the acrobats of the high alpine zone. First observed on June 6 and present to end of season. On June 20 a spectacular series of courtship flights were viewed on the East Cliff of the Cheshnina Gorge about one mile downriver from Cheshnina Falls. In one instance, a pipit was observed to fly straight up to a point above the 5,000' rim of the cliff. Then, in an instant, he folded his wings and dove straight down, continuing to utter his two-note call as he rapidly gained speed. The descent as measured against the cliff wall was in excess of 700 vertical feet. Beyond that the bird passed out of my line of vision. I was continually amazed by the in-flight agility of these birds, and they likewise displayed a curiosity for my activities. They seemed to enjoy taking the wind head-on so as to maintain a stationary position in midair, and they frequently circled around me as I ascended high ridges, pausing in this stationary mode and turning their heads to regard me.

Ransom Saltmarch

Only a few days behind me were the ice fields and glaciers of Alaska's awesome St. Elias Range, the stark beauty, the bitter wind, the blowing snow, the showers of frost from the tent roof, the deadly whiteouts, the heart-breaking labor of sled hauling, the discovery of close friendships.

High above the valley I could see a jet drifting westward. It would cover in 20 minutes distances that it had taken our party 32 days to get over.

Nowhere on earth, I reflected, could a man find contrasts more dramatic or more difficult to understand and assimilate. At that moment my feeling was that of primitive man, mouth agape, gazing in amazement at the twentieth century. Maybe that's what ski and sled travel in ice-locked mountains is all about.

The thing that has always affected me most about wilderness experiences is the profound and unfathomable silence. It is heart-stopping and total. Traveling, one hears his own squeaking and rustling. But at rest stops or on a calm night, when no wind is blowing, there is only a benign silence that bonds man with the land. Nowhere have I known that silence to be more engulfing than on those icefields. . . .

It had snowed as we slept, which meant that the sled hauling would be harder than ever. By evening the silence had closed down again, and the next day a whiteout enveloped our world. Snow and sky turned precisely the same hue, all suggestion of a horizon was eliminated, the mountains vanished, and we navigated by compass, moving on a treadmill, using our ski poles as outriggers to keep our balance, the light so flat that we could not see a crevasse until we stood on its very brink, or make out an incline until our skis tilted up.

. . . we learned to have no expectations. Always the mountains kept the upper hand.

Ned Gillette[4]

We are a diverse and dynamic group of people, no more or less than people anywhere else. Yet it can be said that the sometimes harsh environment in which we live, in which we built our homes, hunt and gather wood has made us keenly aware of the sensitivities and limits of this area. Learning to live with and accept these limits has woven us into the fabric of nature's tapestry just as surely as the animals and trees.

McCarthy Community Council, 1979

We talked with a visitor from Washington, D.C., just after she had finished a rafting trip; she described the experience of a fellow passenger:

It was amazing to see; there was this woman who said at first she wasn't scared — that "Sure, no problem with this trip." But as the trip went on, after two or three days out in the wilderness you could see her change. She really grew a lot and opened herself up to the experience. It was the river and being out there in that extreme environment that did it. We were really scared sometimes. We just got to thinking that we were really way out in the wilds, and if something happened then we'd really be in trouble. It was an unforgettable experience that has changed my mind about this area. It truly is wilderness.

He advised us that the answer to our question of why he was living in the Wrangells had to be answered through our own experiences. "Go take a walk fifteen miles into the wilderness, and go out and see the land, interview a moose. Then perhaps you'll understand why I am here."

D.C. Defenderfer and
Robert B. Walkinshaw[5]

ALASKA NATIONAL PARKLANDS

THE INTERIOR

A place to nurture the myth . . .

The worn uplands of Yukon-Charley bear little resemblance to the new-forged mountains of the Pacific Rim. The rhythm of the country is slower. The long cycles of time are deeply embedded in rocks unmasked by the rivers.

On the frontier between Canada and Alaska, Yukon-Charley combines the majesty of a mighty river and the intimate beauty of tributary streams. The Yukon — here constricted between soaring palisades — drains the greatest mountain systems of North America. Its opaque waters bear glacial silt from a thousand icy peaks. But the Charley River and its sister tributaries flow clear. Their sources in the Yukon-Tanana uplands and the Ogilvie Mountains are too far from the sea to catch the deep snows that make glaciers.

Rimmed by mountains, guarded by its own shoals and rapids, the Charley River has foiled massive assault by man. From alpine headwaters the Charley flows north 88 miles to its junction with the Yukon. Along the way it traverses a broad spectrum of interior Alaska landscapes. Expansive uplands form gigantic tundra-clothed amphitheaters skylined by ragged granite monoliths. Golden eagles and gyrfalcons soar over these sentinel rocks on glide patterns that nicely trace the mountain airs. Caribou trails lace the high ridges.

Imprinted like outstretched hands on the open mountainsides, stream courses descend thousands of feet in sweeping steps to the narrowing midsection of the Charley. Nourished by the streams, sheltered by their lower canyons and gorges, fingers of subalpine forest reach upward to penetrate the tundra slopes.

As the upper tributaries converge, the Charley plunges into a region of cliffs and bluffs. Dall sheep, normally found on mountain crags, are often seen scaling these riverside scarps. In summer, peregrine falcons guard nesting sites hidden in the bluffs' inaccessible crannies. The Charley's crystal waters gain speed and depth as they careen through alternating shadowed and sunlit narrows where Arctic grayling flash. Side streams are bigger here. In flood they slant through forested benchlands, tumbling huge boulders into the Charley to create the white-water rapids that dominate this part of its course.

Wildlife and trapline trails wind through the bordering forests of white spruce, birch, and aspen. Occasional trapper's or hunter's cabins blend into the forest shade. Along the trails, wisps of hair on bushes mark the passage of black bear or grizzly.

Finally the swift waters break from the hills, and the river changes once again. Now it meanders slowly and deeply through a lowland of sloughs, marshes, bogs, and stands of black spruce. This is moose and bald eagle country. Here, too, lurks the northern pike.

Near its outlet the Charley carves into its banks to expose thick lenses of ice, crumbling sections of the permafrost underlying this country. Even in summer, warmth is superficial here.

Debouching into the Yukon, the Charley's clear waters spill forth against the silt and for awhile run bannerlike against the bank. Then they merge and disappear.

The change of tone from Charley to Yukon is profound. From *a* river, one enters *the* river — big, continental, the central artery of a vast Canadian-Alaskan Interior. To be on that river, beyond sounds from either shore, is to experience the timeless present.

Now the landscape loses sharpness and blends into distant horizons. Massive cliffs rise toward mountain backdrops. Skyscapes vary from fair-weather cloud puffs and towering thunderheads to lowering squall-driven nimbus and scud. When rain blots out the shore and spindrift whips the waves, the forested islands float by like ships at sea.

This is the historic environment of steamboats and roadhouses and mining camps, where men seeking gold surged up and down the Yukon, alternating between Canadian and Alaskan strikes.

The upper Yukon today is almost deserted by comparison with the yesteryears of the gold moilers.

Where a few score people now live along its banks —
clinging to its memories or reliving its history — boom
towns once sprang up overnight. Shallow-draft, stern-
wheel steamers plied the river by the hundreds to bring
mail and supplies to the miners and the retinue that
followed them from strike to strike.

Circle City — Paris of the North — boasted an
opera house. Eagle City with its military post, Fort
Egbert, became the center of civil and military
administration in northern Alaska, crossroads of
transportation and supply. The heyday ended quickly
for both towns, but their proud heritage remains.

Along the banks of the Yukon old cabins and camps
molder into encroaching vegetation. Collapsing fish
racks, a broken stove, a child's shoe, old catalogs and
letters and diaries — these are the hints of the people
who once listened for the boat whistle and gathered at a
score of landings for news of a distant world or passage
on the steamer.

Today a string of international parklands and
historic places commemorates those busy days —
Seattle and Skagway, Dawson, Eagle, Circle, and beyond
to the Bering Sea.

The search for riches still goes on. In the Yukon-
Charley region and on other streams and creeks can be
found the last holdouts of a past century — prospectors
and trappers who would be right at home with
Klondike's discoverers. Some search for metal; others
seek the peace and beauty of a remote and timeless
land.■

[Eagle and Circle] are about a hundred and sixty
river miles apart, and in all the land between them live
perhaps thirty people. The State of New Jersey, where I
happen to live, could fit between Eagle and Circle. New
Jersey has seven and a half million people. Small
wonder that the Alaskan wild has at least a conceptual
appeal to certain people from a place like New Jersey.
John McPhee[1]

The mythic frontier has been just as important as the real one in shaping the American experience. The Yukon River and its tributaries, still seemingly pristine, provide a place to nurture the myth on terms that the land imposes. It is this concept of a historical environment that lends cohesion to the geography of Yukon-Charley and the experiences of its visitors.

Melody Webb[2]

Fifty years ago in the twilight of the goldrush, wagon roads and freight trails were still in use here. Though they are badly overgrown now and deeply rutted, I can still walk parts of them for a short distance.... It is strange to think of it then, the country still busy with people coming and going, the dogs and horses, freight and men....

I am living out a dream in these woods. Old dreams of the Far North, old stories read and absorbed: of snow and dogs, of moose and lynx, and of all that is still native to these unpeopled places. Nothing I have yet done in life pleases me as much as this. And yet it seems only half-deliberate, as if I had followed a scent on the wind and found myself in this place. Having come, I will have to stay, there's no way back.

John Haines[3]

My wife and I hunt, fish, trap and live year round in the Nation River area of Yukon-Charley. We came into the country in June of '74 with one dog, one 17' canoe and no money; and since then we have learned how to subsist in the bush. We fish for salmon in the Yukon in summer, and hunt and trap the Nation drainage in winter. We live at different locations (cabins and tent camps) determined by seasonal changes in fur, fish and game populations. Over the years we have acquired more dogs (we now have five) and a larger canoe with a 10 hp motor to help move our outfit around. Mobility is the key to subsistence. I have come to know and love this country very much and I feel I am taking proper care of it as I must in order that it continue to support us.

David Evans

The Yukon is a practical thoroughfare in summer and in winter, but during its times of transition it becomes almost unapproachably inimical. Great floes coming on from upriver roll, heave, compile; sound and surface like whales. Many hundreds of millions of tons of ice, riding a water discharge of two hundred thousand cubic feet per second, go by Eagle at a speed approaching ten miles an hour. Looking at the river, you cannot help but recoil. In water that cold, a human couldn't live much more than a few minutes — a benevolent brevity, the struggle being hopeless anyway against the current and the ice....

The ice run will thin out now and again, nearly disappear. The river becomes clear of all but isolated floes. In another hour, or day, heavy ice is running again — wall to wall, crunching, jamming, lethal as ever. The ice comes segmentally from upriver and from the tributary rivers. The Yukon, even above Eagle, has tributaries four hundred miles long. When ice of the Yukon, ice of the tributaries comes free and begins to run, it does so in big units.... The White, the Klondike, the Stewart, the Pelly, the Nordenskiold, the Teslin, the Fortymile let go their ice arrhythmically and give it into the Yukon. Pelly ice. Stewart ice. Teslin ice. Fortymile ice. It takes two or three weeks for it all to go by a single point like Eagle.

We picked our way through flights of wooded islands. We shivered in the deep shadows of bluffs a thousand feet high — Calico Bluff, Montauk Bluff, Biederman Bluff, Takoma Bluff — which day after day intermittently walled the river. Between them — in downpourings of sunshine, as often as not — long vistas reached back across spruce-forested hills to the rough gray faces and freshly whitened summits of mountains.

Some of the walls of the bluffs were of dark igneous rock that had cracked into bricks and appeared to have been set there by masons. . . . Peregrine falcons nest there, and — fantastic flyers — will come over the Yukon at ballistic speeds, clench their talons, tuck them in, and strike a flying duck hard enough (in the neck) to kill it in midair. End over end the duck falls, and the falcon catches it before it hits the river. . . .

John McPhee[4]

In 1911, the river steamer was queen. There was a great fleet then, nearly all with feminine names, churning and chuffing their stern wheels up the rivers and sliding briskly down them. . . . Back in those times "the last trip of the year" was no meaningless phrase. It meant that all the supplies for the community, enough to last until "the first boat in the spring" came, had to be already delivered and safely stored away in the warehouses and stores — and everyone hoped he hadn't forgotten to order something important.

There is one thing gone forever from our world — the irrevocability of those departures, before the age of the airplane. This was the last boat, and Nature would take over from now until the middle of June.

Margaret Murie[5]

The approach of winter along the Yukon is heralded by the falling and partial clearing of the water in the river, due to the freezing of the smaller tributaries and feeders in the hills. This is followed by the formation of ice in the sloughs and the slack-water places along the main river, and soon after by the appearance of floating ice in the channel. The period of floating ice varies from two to four weeks, final closing occuring, according to two years' observation and inquiry upon this subject, at very nearly the same time each year.

Capt. W. P. Richardson, 1899

On January 2, the thermometer registered 62 degrees below zero. In weather as cold as that, when one exhales the breath, the moisture congeals instantly, and a distinct pop can be heard. It is practically impossible for wind to blow at this temperature. If it did, it would freeze you just the way a hot iron burns.

Having a long nose that protruded whenever it had a chance and was constantly being frozen on the end, I hit upon the scheme of putting a little piece of snowshoe rabbit fur on it, the hairs of which stick out about an inch and a half. The moisture from my face held it there.

Ice formed all over our parka hoods from the moisture of our breath and had to be knocked off every little while. Long beards and mustaches become instantly caked with ice, and are not only an inconvenience but a menace, as they might freeze one's face. That is why men in the North shave clean in winter, after having let their beards grow long in the summer to keep the mosquitoes off.

Lt. William Mitchell, 1902

White people who first came into the interior knew very little of the country or how to live or travel in it. There were no road houses nor any places in which to live, other than what the Indians could furnish. The Indians harbored them and helped them in many ways. They took care of the white men, provided them with food, etc. Things continued in this way several years, the effect of which, on a people like the Indians, whose margin of existence is always small, was to make them very poor.

David Jarvis, Eagle City, 1903

During the winter season [the Han Indians] moved about wherever game is plentiful. The men go to a place, cache their packs, and then proceed to hunt. The next day the women come, pitch the camp, and prepare to cook. In the spring they go to the river bank, where they make canoes and nets in preparation for salmon fishing, and during the summer dry and cache large quantities of fish. In the early fall the entire family goes hunting and when a good supply of game is accumulated they cache it on the spot. In October they return to the river for about two months, when they make snow-shoes, toboggans, and other things for winter use. About the middle of January they have a big time — 'all same Christmas' — when they get out all their cached meat and bring it to the river. They stay there till the meat is nearly gone, and again go in search of game until the middle of March, when the weather moderates, at which time they return to the river banks.

Ferdinand Schmitter, 1910

I think the one hundred and seventy-five or one hundred and eighty miles of river from Eagle to Circle would be counted exceedingly picturesque anywhere in the world. Each bend brings a change in the composition; now the sharp peaks of the Sheep Creek mountains dominate the scene, now the enormous bulk of the cliffs below Nation, now the lofty tableland of the bluffs opposite Washington Creek.

Hudson Stuck, 1917

That winter John Williams and I decided to put in the winter prospecting on the 70-mile at Barney Creek. I took up a pack load of provisions in late September, a hard trip across the hills, siwashing out two nights in six inches of snow. Saw no game of any kind. October 25th the creeks were frozen fairly well so we took my dog, "Whiskers" with 150 lbs. on the sled and we made it in four days to Barney Creek. It was tough going. I helped the dog pull the sled. Williams was 70 years old and not able to do that kind of work. We stayed at Barney Creek on the 70-Mile in a small one room cabin and put down 16 holes to bed-rock, all by hand, with wood fire. Bed rock was from 2 to 26 ft. deep, according to location. No pay in most of them but 3 holes showed 10 to 25 cents to the pan on bed rock and 12 ft. deep. Whiskers helped to haul the wood. We melted ice for water, had caribou meat. Whiskers lived on rabbits which were plentiful. We put in a pleasant winter. No financial results but a lot of valuable experience.

C. A. Bryant, 1913[6]

Then there was Nimrod Robertson, known as the man who could make anything but a living, and this was correct. He would divide his last dollar with you; fix anything you had broken whether it be a watch or axe handle, gratis. He was a genius. He is the man who pulled his own teeth, made a set out of a bear's teeth and then ate the bear. . . .

December 7th letter from Charles Ott of Eagle gave me a shock. . . . Nimrod . . . had frozen to death on the trail between 70-Mile and Eagle. His body was found by Gus Douglas and Charles Bierderman. . . .

It came about in this way. He had gone down the Yukon in his boat to the mouth of the 70-Mile, in October, to look at some placer ground, which he had staked in early summer, and he intended to stay but a few days. It turned cold suddenly in early November. The ice was running too heavy and he could not get back that way. His provisions were exhausted. He started across country to Eagle, 20 miles, by an old trail which had not been used since 1900. He was so weak and worn out he could go no further although he had made nearly half way. He could not get his fire to burn and was likely numb with cold. He realized his time had come. He stood his rifle against a tree, hung his field glasses on a bush, lay down and pulled his parka hood over his face, folded his arms and dropped to sleep, never to wake until Judgment Day. It was a peaceful ending for he did not stir from that position. He was past 84 years.

C. A. Bryant, 1940

The Yukon-Charley area, like other parts of the earth, is the result of an incredibly complex skein of events which have taken place over an almost inconceivably long period of time. The distinctive feature here is the clarity with which so many of these events have been recorded and displayed. The most ancient rocks are giving information on the dawn of life itself, while other deposits may tell us about the early history of the flowering plants, the rise of the tundra biome, or the history of the early human inhabitants of North America and the fate of their now extinct mammalian contemporaries.

Steve Young[7]

In terms of occurrence in a relatively small geographic area, completeness of depositional record, and persistent presence of fossils, this area is unique in America. In fact, search for a comparable record elsewhere, based on these criteria, failed to locate a single candidate in the world.

Carol Allison[8]

The valley of the Charley is a totally undeveloped and undefiled wild area. The river winds in giant curves through mountain country of impressive but not awesome proportions. For three days, we drifted in the warm sunlight down its limpid course, shooting its rapids, gazing at the golden rocks and pebbles on its bottom, drinking its cold purity, taking its grayling for dinner, climbing its mountainsides through colorful mosses and wild flowers, scattered spruces and birches, marveling at its magnificent vistas, its eagles, falcons and mountain sheep.

John Seiberling[9]

SOME YEARS WINTER COMES EARLY
Stomping through autumn
He carries darkness in one hand
Silence in the other
Under his arms are bundles
Of shadows
He stalks through the forest,
Throws down his burdens
With his hands he spreads darkness
In the high branches
Scatters silence along the ground
Smooths it around the roots of trees.

SOME YEARS WINTER PAUSES
At the edge of the forest,
Waiting to enter.
His shadow is Darkness
His voice is Silence
His breath a white moon through the trees
His arms are folded across his chest.

NOW WE ARE A FOREST
Winter, Darkness, and Silence come
Hand in hand; they skip around us,
Invite us to dance with them
In a circle. We lay aside colors
And music, then raising our arms
We freeze in our places like trees.

THIS FOREST IS CANDLES
When Darkness comes
Arm in arm with Winter
She bows before each bright tree
Then blows it out with a whisper.

Winter lays silence like a stone
Against each trunk.

Gary Holthaus[10]

This great banner of a mountain . . .

Mount McKinley, looming above the Alaska plain and towering over its consort, Mount Foraker, symbolizes the idea of Alaska. Its lonely eminence, its massive glaciers and great granite buttresses and gorges, its wind-warped arctic summit make it an object both beautiful and dreadful. It stands like a god, and was so conceived and called — Denali, the Great One — by Indians who dwelt in its shadow. Early maps left blank the hundreds of miles of its approaches. Explorers on the fringes of those unknown spaces noted "distant stupendous mountains" or "great ice peaks." One traveler spoke of a "cloud-like summit far in the interior."

From its peak more than 20,000 feet above the sea — rising abruptly 18,000 feet above the plain — the mountain falls away past towers, ridges, and domes toward huge glacial canyons. Walls of rock many thousands of feet high overlook the basins and passes carved in the granite. Crevasses and icefalls mark the stresses and gradients of the glaciers, which never melt in the perpetual winter of the higher elevations. Below the fields of ice and snow, bare rocky valleys lead to tundra plateaus. From there the descent continues to wide valley floors traversed by braided glacial rivers and parallel bands of boreal forest. On the steps and benches bordering the floodplains, lakes and ponds dot the landscape and reflect the mountain vistas.

A convocation of wildlife roams the vast lowlands more than 3 miles below Denali's summit. In this big, wide country — backdropped as far as the eye can see by the elegant structure of the Alaska Range — the animals blend into folds of landscape, moss-floored forest, and distant fields of tundra. Seasonally, caribou and sheep come together in migrating bands. Foraging bear and moose families roam the slopes and stream courses, packing away food, building the reserves of fat to carry them through winter. Fortunate is the viewer who crosses the paths of these wanderers. Seen or unseen, the animals are always there. It is a place full of surprise and uncertainty. At any moment, around any bend, a creature of wild and regal beauty may suddenly be there.

On the northwest side of the range — between the high mountains and parallel foothills — lies a great valley crossed by a score of major drainages that originate in the high glaciers. A road penetrates the heart of the wildlife sanctuary through this lowland. From the road, hikers can leave the human world for the natural pathways that follow river, canyon, and ridge. Tracks in sand and mud alert the senses to the company of animals at large in their world.

Winter is never far away at Denali. It is constant in the high mountains; in the lowlands it has just left or is coming on fast. The explosion of warm-weather life and activity has two purposes: to perpetuate the species and to fuel individual plants and animals for survival of eight months of winter that kills the weak and unprepared. Most birds simply fly away. The living things that stay must go dormant, living on stored energy, or be so tough that they can run the merciless gauntlet of cold, wind, and dark hunger and still come out alive the next spring.

The greenery of summer shades quickly into scarlet, bronze, and gold. Animals rush their eating, spurred by warning chemistries that keep pace with the chemistry of plants as they change from florescence to dormancy. The brilliant colors of the dying leaves temporarily warm landscapes soon to be dim and frozen.

Responding to the tireless efforts of Charles Sheldon, Congress established Mount McKinley National Park in 1917. Sheldon, a wealthy hunter and student of wildlife, had visited the wilderness of Denali several times, wintering over in 1907-08 in a cabin on the Toklat River. Depredations by commercial meat hunters had convinced him that this great wildlife range would be lost unless protected. Sheldon's guide during the early

visits, Harry Karstens, became the park's first superintendent. Karstens was a tough Sourdough who had mined, carried mail, and explored from Eagle to Kantishna. In 1913, he, Hudson Stuck, and their Indian companion Walter Harper, were the first to stand on Mount McKinley's summit. Karstens established a tradition of wilderness self-reliance still evident in the winter dog-team patrols and backcountry studies by park rangers and naturalists in Alaska.

Boundaries of the 1917 park encompassed only parts of the Mount McKinley massif, along with the great valley to the northwest. The Alaska Lands Act of 1980 redesignated the area Denali National Park and Preserve and enlarged it to include the mountain's southeast flanks and glacier gorges, the sheer granite Cathedral Spires, and a westerly extension of tundra, lakes, foothills, and forest that protects the wildlife ecosystem. The landmark biological studies of Adolph Murie, beginning in the 1920s, laid the base for the new boundaries.

Alfred Hulse Brooks in 1902 led the first exploratory survey along the north face of the Alaska Range. He recorded the sentiments of his party as it approached its goal: " . . . we lent ourselves readily to the influence of the clear, invigorating air and the inspiration of that majestic peak ever looming before us, the highest mountain of North America." After scrambling up a few thousand feet where ice blocked his further ascent, he "gazed along the precipitous slopes of the mountain and tried to realize again its great altitude." Thus has Denali always moved those fortunate to look upon it. Artists give their best efforts to its depiction. Mountaineers respond to its physical challenge, seeking, in Brooks' words, "the broad vision denied those at lower altitudes." For most of us, it is enough simply to contemplate the constantly changing moods and perspectives of this solitary giant, so far aloft in its shifting shroud of cloud streamers. ■

courtesy of the Mary Whalen Collection, 75-84-490, University of Alaska, Fairbanks

December 26. Morning temperature 31 degrees below. It was my purpose to spend this day about the base of Denali. Fog hung low when I rose before daylight, and although it continued, I started up the river bed. On the snow-covered moraine wolverine tracks were everywhere abundant, and old moose tracks were plentiful among the stunted willows along the river and elsewhere for three miles above the timber. After proceeding four miles I found myself above the fog. Denali, immaculately clear, towered above me, its lower slopes crossed by a thin band of pink vapor, the sky above it pink, yellow, gold, crimson, of ever-changing color tones. Conies were bleating all about on the moraine, and willow ptarmigan were abundant. A chickadee flitted among the uppermost willows, and old tracks of a small band of sheep, coming from the outside mountain to the west, crossed the moraine toward the eastern foothills.

Great avalanches continually kept falling with crashing sounds that rolled among the outside ranges. The river near the glacier was open and the murmur of its current was audible though subdued. The whole vast north face of Denali was mutilated by avalanches, exposing the underlying black rock. The great mountain rose above me desolate, magnificent, overpowering. The lower ranges were white, while below, nothing could be seen but the fog, which took on the appearance of thick clouds. I felt, as never before, completely alone in the presence of this mighty mountain; no words can describe my feelings.

Charles Sheldon, 1906[1]

... this great banner of a mountain, with its heraldic display of wildlife ...

John Kauffmann

... after we had relayed every thing we wanted up to the glacier we broke camp leaving one tent pitched and proceded up the glacier to very near 8000 ft. level, about 5 miles above where we first struck the glacier and here is where I had to solve the problem of glacier travel ... I had to figer out bridging crevasses, good snow from bad snow. Ice bridges Natural & home made, it surely is some interesting .... from the 8000 to 9000 there was a large serack to go over with many crevasses on it ranging from a foot to 50 feet wide, some were open and others covered with light drifted snow a slight touch and it breaks through. we would sprinkle snow on them till strong enough to bear blocks of snow & build an arched bridge which would hold like a stone wall. other places we would find blocks of Ice which had broken off and fallen half way across which would serve as a bridge. then emagin the grim Icey ridge on eather side with hanging glaciers discharging ice every few moments ... 11500 the head of the Muldrough & the foot of the great N.E. Ridge which leads up to the upper basin between the two peaks. "0" it is a great sight a great basin a mile wide with towering cliffs on all sides but down the glacier, and a low saddle 500 ft. high in the N.E. ridge all covered with hanging glaciers and the great Ice falls coming out from between the two peaks and dropping ice a shere 4000 feet every 15 or 20 minutes. sometimes a great mass would break loose from a spur of the North peak goodness knows how many thousand feet ... here is where we had our worst weather. we camped here three weeks, again & again Walter & I tackled the ridge, fogs & storms would drive us back and every time we went we had to shovel steps out ... you can hardly emagine what a proposition that ridge was ... when we tackled it it was a jumbled up mass of ice, Knife edge in places ... blocks of ice in others. some balancing on the ridge, 2 blows of my axe sent one as big as a two story house crashing and roring into the basin thousands of feet below ... cutting the top of the ridge off to make a path with almost shere drops on eather side untill we found a fairly flat place on the ridge at 13000. here we first used our small tent and oil stove. for five hundred feet above us it was terrably jagged and torn and then a sharp cleavage up onto a snow slope which lead to the 15000 foot level and here was the hardest and most dangerous of them all getting up onto this snow slope, it was 50 ft shere from top of ridge to top of snow slope and no chance of cutting steps up, so I cut down the base of the clevage along some drifted snow, every once in a while cutting a good foot hold in the ice so in case the snow gave away there was something to hold to . . . we gained the snow slope and found it rather steeper than we suposed but easy going compared to what was behind, after climbing up the snow slope (cutting steps all the way) about 1000 feet we where driven back by a storm, but next day we made the 15000 foot level, the edge of the upper basin. we were above the storms, the next two days we spent in relaying our camp and provisions up. . . .

The next morning after we made camp at 18000 was a fine one. none of us slept that night. we pulled aut at 4 A.M. and reached the top at 1 P.M. Fine clear sunshinie day & a stiff wind blowing, thermometer recorded 4 above and it was some cold . . . we pitched a little tent I made for to read the instruments in. read the instruments, said a little prayer, erected a cross, took a few Photos, looked around a little and started down. 1 hour & 1/2 was all we could stand it. . . . We reached the top of the Mt. on June 7, 1913, 1 P.M. and reached our base camp June 9th 10 P.M. What a change the smell of flowers & green things, every thing in summer bloom, it is hard for me to express. we laid over in base camp one day to clear up then packed dogs & our selves & started for Eureka which took two days in pouring rain. when I seen Hamilton I yelled for coffee & mush & plenty of it with lots of sugar and got it. I nearly foundered myself. I had lost 20 lbs. on trip . . .

Harry Karstens[2]

I sit and think, why am I here? Why am I going to try to climb Denali? Perhaps it is because Mt. McKinley frightens me so and is a symbol of my other fears. It rises above, seemingly unconquerable. Climbers such as I are powerless before it, unable to control where it will throw down avalanches, open crevasses, spread unseen cold or buckle us to our knees in high wind and blizzards. We are completely at its mercy, as we tred up its slopes.

I first saw it in 1976 and have been haunted by it since. I must search for myself on its air-barren summit. I am here because I am afraid and must conquer my fear.

R. Bruce Duncan[3]

During the three years I worked under the supervision of Karstens, I found him to be very fair and considerate. I made several long trips into the back country of the Park with him, and he taught me many original ways of getting along the trail.

On several occasions during the time I was at the park Karstens actually came to blows with some of the park personnel, and I never knew him to come out second best.

Considering that he was in a frontier area, he was a realistic administrator. Those were the days when a Ranger was not required to pass a Civil Service Examination. He had his own system, and considering the type of duties a Ranger was required to perform, his system certainly weeded out those who were unfit for the job.

When I talked to Karstens about a Ranger's job, he asked me a number of questions about my experience as a woodsman and wilderness man.

I shall never forget that, when he got through asking questions, he said, "You're lacking in experience, but I think you can learn. I'll send you on a patrol trip alone. You will be gone a week. If you don't get back by then, I'll come looking for you, and you had better have plans made for a new job. Now this is what I want you to do." He then outlined a week's patrol trip cross-country through territory new to me. There were no blazed trails to follow. One could follow only the terrain cross-country. He also gave me a rough map and much valuable advice. No reliable maps of the Park were available in those days.

Karstens said, "This will be a trial trip, and real test for you. We can't use anyone on our Ranger force who can't take care of himself in the wilds.

"The Ranger you are replacing was unfit for this service. We sent him out on the same patrol you are going to make and he returned in a most pitiful condition. He just staggered back, almost starved. The poor fellow was gone for three days and couldn't find the patrol cabin. He hadn't eaten a hot meal since he left. His reason was that he couldn't find any water that wasn't frozen to ice. The ground was covered with snow. He had a trail axe and could have cut some dry wood and melted ice or snow for water. Luckily the weather was warm, about zero and he didn't suffer any frostbite.

"When this fellow took the job he said he had plenty of experience out in the wilderness by himself. This trip you are making isn't too tough. However, it is the kind that separates the glamour boys from the type we can use in our work."

Grant Pearson[4]

On the third day we set off along Igloo Creek in a pouring rain. Just below Sable Pass we headed southward toward the mountains. On the divide above the East Fork we stopped for lunch and to graze the horses. The sun came out, and a gentle warm breeze tossed the myriad wildflowers that carpeted the tundra. Below us to the southwest, a glacier lay, squeezed between towering pinnacles partially hidden by clouds. We watched a large blond grizzly pawing the tundra a half mile away. A short distance beyond him, oblivious of his presence, grazed a band of mountain sheep. Herds of caribou trotted along a ridge east of us, bent on some predetermined destination. It was as tho the essence of the northland had been distilled for us at this spot this afternoon.

Woody, who has waded so many glacier streams, chuckled with glee as our horses carried us dry-footed

courtesy of the National Park Service

to the opposite bank of the East Fork River. It was here that we began to realize that the herds of caribou we had been seeing were not just casual bands. We were in the middle of an early migration! For the next 40 miles we became a part of the ceaseless onward movement of thousands of caribou. From time to time a few, especially curious calves, would bound up to within a hundred feet of us, then leap away when they discovered we were not one of them. But most of the time they paid little attention to us. Together we slogged across the boggy tundra, splashed across glacier streams, filed up valleys and spread out across tundra flats. We had witnessed many a caribou migration in the park, but this was the first time we had participated in one. All night long they passed by our tents while we waited for one to trip on a guy rope and collapse our shelters.

Ginny Hill Wood & Celia Hunter, 1960[5]

Even without [the mountain, the park] would be outstanding because of its alpine scenery, its arctic vegetation, and its wildlife. I have walked over the green, flowering slopes in the rain, when the fog hid the landscape beyond a few hundred yards, and felt that the white mountain avens, the purple rhododendrons, and the delicate white bells of the heather at my feet were alone worthy of our efforts.

Adolph Murie[6]

The national park idea represents a far-reaching cultural achievement, for here we raise our thoughts above the average, and enter a sphere in which the intangible values of the human heart and spirit take precedence. Mingled with the landscape of McKinley Park is the spirit of the primeval. . . .

All the plants and animals enjoy a natural and normal life without human restrictions. Freedom prevails — the foxes are free to dig burrows where they will; to hunt ptarmigan, ground squirrels and mice as the spirit moves; and they share in the ownership of the blueberry and crowberry patches. The grizzlies wander over their ancestral home unmolested; dig roots and ground squirrels, graze grass, and harvest berries according to whatever menu appeals to them. The "bad" wolf seeks an honest living as of yore; he is a respected citizen, morally on a par with everyone else. His hunting of mice, ground squirrels, caribou and Dall sheep is his way of life and he has the freedom to follow it. No species of plant is favored above the rest, and they grow together, quietly competing, or living in adjusted composure. Our task is to perpetuate this freedom and purity of nature, this ebb and flow of life — first, by insuring ample park boundaries so that the region is large enough to maintain the natural relationships, and secondly, to hold man's intrusions to the minimum.

Adolph Murie[7]

On the flat the wolf stopped for a moment, and so did all the caribou. . . . Then the wolf seemed to come to a decision, for he started after twenty-five cows and calves farther from him than those he had been chasing. Before they got under way he gained rapidly, but soon they were fleeing.

For a time the race seemed to be going quite evenly, and I felt sure the band would outdistance their enemy; but I was mistaken. The gap commenced to close, at first almost imperceptibly. The wolf was stretched out, long and sinewy, doing his best. Then I noticed a calf dropping behind the fleeing band. It could not keep the pace. The space between the calf and the band increased, while that between the calf and the wolf decreased. The calf began to lose ground more rapidly. The wolf seemed to increase his speed a notch and rapidly gained on the calf. When about ten yards ahead of the wolf, the calf began to veer from one side to the other to dodge him. Quickly, the wolf closed in and at the moment of contact the calf went down. I could not be sure where the wolf seized it, but it appeared to be about at the shoulder. The chase had covered about five hundred yards and the victim was about fifty yards behind the herd when overtaken.

*

The snow on the ground made it easy to backtrack the chase. The story was simple. The two ewes and a lamb had been feeding on *Equisetum* on a broad, moist swale not far above Igloo Creek. (The stomach contents of the two victims were made up mainly of *Equisetum*.) The wolves had been following along the mountain slope at a level slightly higher than that where the sheep fed. Coming over a rise, they spied the sheep feeding in the swale 150 yards below them. The tracks showed that the wolves did not start running until they were within seventy-five yards of the sheep. The latter galloped out of the swale and ran down-ward at an angle toward Igloo Creek, which they crossed after descending a steep dirt bank about a hundred feet high. The wolves followed directly after the sheep, but instead of running among the large rocks in the canyon stream bed as the sheep had done, they ran alongside the rocks on the smoother ground covered with a sod of avens. Two hundred fifty yards up this creek the two ewes were captured just before reaching some cliffs. The lamb escaped, and . . . we saw it alone a short distance above the carcasses. The ewes had run half a mile before the capture.

*

I had many opportunities to observe the interesting habits of the sheep while they were migrating to and from the purely summer ranges. Before venturing to cross over low intervening country, the sheep may spend hours looking over the region from the slopes, apparently to be sure the coast is clear. Sometimes they spend a day or two watching before making the attempt. Often ewes and rams move across together in a compact band. . . .

On June 7, 1940, a band of about sixty-four sheep, both ewes and rams, crossed from Sanctuary Canyon to the low hills adjoining Double Mountain. They started crossing about two P.M. and did not arrive at the hills until five-thirty. Most of the way the sheep traveled in a compact group, stopping frequently to look ahead. Through tall willows and scattered spruce woods they walked in single file. Just before reaching the first hills, they fed for about forty-five minutes on the flats at their base. They probably were hungry and came upon some choice food. When they emerged from the woods to the open hills, they were strung out considerably and galloped up the slope in high spirits, seeming relieved to have made the crossing.

Adolph Murie[8]

As I traveled over the lowland and up the outer slopes of the mountains, I enjoyed recording what I saw. I was pleased to see the chickadee among the lower branches of a spruce, always busy and much alive, adding a cheery note to any winter woods. This bird often came to the spruces near the trail, as if he too were glad to see someone. There was also the magpie, always aloof and wary. . . . His dark body with striking stripes and patches of white gave a vivacious accent to the winter landscape. Then there were the tracks in the snow — tracks of squirrels, tiny shrews, and snowshoe hares. I knew there were wolverines, for now and then I saw the tracks of this elusive animal, too. At night I sometimes heard the great horned owl. All of this made me aware that underneath the apparent lifelessness in this wintry northland the landscape was still alive.

*

field sketch by Olaus Murie courtesy of M. E. Murie

Now, in retrospect, I want to be back again, with a loaded sled creaking its way over rough ice or running smoothly and quietly over level places, with a good team of dogs trotting steadily in front, muzzles low, tails waving high — and the snow stretching away until broken by the blue line of woods where we might camp for the night.

Olaus Murie[9]

Then I heard a familiar cry — it was the sky music of sandhill cranes in migration. I scanned the upper atmosphere hurriedly, for I wanted to watch the cranes as long as possible before they should pass by and disappear into the distant blue to the south. So high do they sometimes fly that it often requires some looking into higher altitudes to discover them. More clarion notes, now more distinct as the flock came nearer, and then I discovered the V-shaped lines of the cranes following along the crest of the Alaska Range. To the major V formation of the flock were joined subsidiary lines forming subsidiary V's. Behind these were small, independent V patterns, all integral parts of the flock, numbering about four hundred. And as these birds moved majestically eastward past the top of Denali, some 20,300 feet in elevation, I discovered other large skeins in their wake, westward as far as the eye would take me. Flock after flock was flying along the mountains, some just behind the peaks of Denali, some over the top, and still others on the near side, silhouetted against the snow-white mountain. . . .

Apparently the recent rainy weather had grounded many flocks, which today were all well fed and poised for southward flight in the clear weather. Cranes which had been widely spaced in their nesting activities, some in western Alaska, others in Siberia, were in more simultaneous flight than I had ever witnessed. As a biologist I should have meticulously counted the cranes, but prosaic counting today seemed a sacrilegious thing. I did count quickly the cranes in a few flocks and estimated the number of flocks, but only roughly, and I guessed that five or six thousand had taken part in this adventure.

field sketch by Olaus Murie courtesy of M. E. Murie

I recall the first bear track I ever saw. It was my initial day afield in McKinley Park and my brother and I were crossing from Jenny Creek over a rise to Savage River, on our way to the head of the river. One lone track in a patch of mud is all we saw. But the track was a symbol, and more poetic than seeing the bear himself — a delicate and profound approach to the spirit of the Alaska Wilderness. A bear track at any time may create a stronger emotion than the old bear himself, for the imagination is brought into play. You examine the landscape sharply, expecting a bear on every slope as your quickened interest becomes eager and enterprising. The bear is somewhere, and may be anywhere. The country has come alive with a new, rich quality.

Adolph Murie[10]

ALASKA NATIONAL PARKLANDS

THE FAR NORTH

This northbound pilgrimage ends in the Arctic. Here is completed the long transition from known to unknown, from temperate, wooded zones to frigid, shelterless barrens. The Arctic is the far reach of the Earth, the extremity at the end of its tilted axis, on the verge of the cold abyss that sucks heat from fragile life. Beyond the shelter of the trees the atmosphere seems thin and outer space too near. Severe climate, austere form, and spare life distinguish this region from the temperate parts of the world.

Far North parklands extend from Chukchi Sea and Seward Peninsula to the central Brooks Range. Four great river systems drain the western half of this mountain wilderness. The rivers mark gradations of climate and vegetative cover created by the topographic barrier of the east-west range: On the south flank, Koyukuk and Kobuk flow through forested valleys at the northern limit of the continental treeline. Farther north, Noatak and Colville course through tundra and brush, their wide valleys covered with wind-packed snow in winter. To the west, along the shoreline of Cape Krusenstern and across the exposed lowlands of Seward Peninsula, constant winds combine with cold to stunt all growth. Beyond the shores, pack ice migrates south in winter, changing the sea to a solid, though shifting terrain of ridged and tumbled ice.

The geologic history of the region has produced diverse landscapes and startling scenic contrasts. Sand dunes in the Kobuk Valley ripple against a skyline of hyperborean peaks. Hot springs amidst lava flows on the Seward Peninsula prolong summer in oases surrounded by encroaching winter. Tundra flowers bloom over ice lenses that preserve the remains of wooly mammoths.

Effects of the Ice Age are everywhere: In plants and animals common to Alaska and Siberia, from the time of the Bering Land Bridge; in the frozen substrate of land and sea, often thousands of feet thick; in frost-heave hills called pingos; in polygonal ground patterns caused by ice wedges; in the profusion of thaw lakes filling ground depressions left by melted ice.

The Brooks Range — its many mountain groups dominating most of the region — is old in its roots, new in its recently uplifted rugged profile. Its ancient marine sediments have been metamorphosed and intruded by molten masses, then squeezed into tight folds and sliced by faults into sheets that have been shuffled together like a deck of cards. Only a few million years ago it emerged as a high mountainous section, immediately beset by erosion and glaciation to produce today's sawtoothed terrain.

The membrane of life is stretched thin in this place of attenuated heat and interrupted light. Living things proliferate in sunny regions. They expand and expose themselves in the balmy latitudes. But in the Arctic, life seeks cover and distills itself for survival. Plants hug the ground, sheltering themselves in miniature thickets and forests. Animals burrow into insulating snow. They array themselves in tough hides, layers of fat, thick fur, and downy feathers. So adapted and equipped, this well-honed biome faces the combined assaults of wind, cold, and drought — for the Arctic is a desert.

Arctic summer's brevity and 24-hour daylight ignite a frantic perpetuation of life. Migrations of birds and caribou, seals and whales produce momentary concentrations of creatures at other times scattered, some to distant continents and tropic seas. Plants and insects telescope the processes of life — taking days to accomplish the work of seasons elsewhere. The sudden and complete onset of winter brings unremitting hardship and darkness. Plants and the animals that stay hunker down. The others flee with an anxiety that shows. There is nothing more charged with urgency than a tardy flock of plovers winging south past a snow-blown beach as the pack ice closes in.

Into this world came man, possibly 30,000 years ago. Hunting groups traversed the dry steppelands that formed lobes and corridors amongst the glaciers and ice sheets of higher elevations. Moving southward during warmer periods when the ice barriers opened, most of the migrants left the Arctic. But some stayed. Archeological sites trace a series of cultures, each one finely adapted to the climate and prey of its time.

Ancestors of the modern Eskimo became adept at both marine and terrestrial hunting, varying emphasis between the two as climatic cycles and faunal adjustments dictated. Sea ice became a human environment. Complex seal-hunting techniques evolved on the ice — perhaps with clues from the canny polar bear, whose intricate stalk and kill of the seal seems almost preternatural in its foresight. Arctic weather demanded ingenuity in the design of clothes and shelter. Knowledge of ice, wind, and current meant life. Ignorance or carelessness brought sudden death by freezing or wasting away by starvation on the moving pack ice. Inland, the caribou sustained roving bands of communal hunters who traded the warm deer skins to their coastal cousins for seal oil — itself a prime source of warmth as fuel and food.

Ever-expanding knowledge of the environment — born of experience and endless critique of methods and technology — allowed the Eskimo to survive and prosper from Siberia to Greenland. It is this concept of environmental knowledge that distinguishes Eskimo culture. Blessed with only the simplest materials — stone and bone, hide and sinew — these people used their highly trained senses, mental prowess, and infinitely precise language to avert the dangers that stalked them continually and to wrest a living from this difficult part of the world.

Until the recent past, visitors from the south fared well or badly in this unforgiving region, depending on how quickly they learned Eskimo techniques of survival, travel, and hunting. In winter's extremes the same rules apply today for those who leave the temperate-zone compounds built by modern technology.

Despite its forbidding qualities, this Far North country is alive with beauty, much of it gaunt and primordial, but much of it warm and animate — as the waving arctic poppies in sun-drenched coves and valleys. An old man of the Kobuk, who has known its best and its worst, suggests "Maybe we should just leave it like it is."

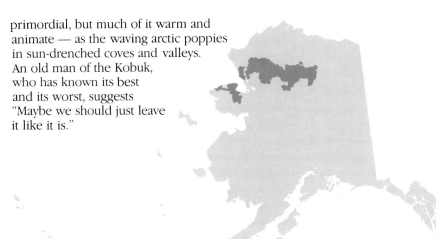

A scale that befits the grandeur...

The central Brooks Range of Alaska stands as the nation's ultimate wilderness. Unknown by outsiders until recent times, this arctic region is still virtually intact and untrammeled. Remote canyons, rugged peaks, wild rivers, pristine lakes, and vast herds of caribou seem all but lost in its expanse. Vast and austere, stern, stark, and uncompromising, yet possessed of haunting beauty, it offers that total immersion in wilderness that has ever been an essential part of life in the New World.

The strange beauty of the Gates of the Arctic country is not easily described, nor are its effects upon the human spirit. The land seems forbidding at first; but as the body toughens and spirits rise, time stops, space expands, humility and confidence grow together. The Arctic's everchanging suffusion of light bathes solitudes that once seemed ominous. The embroidery of wild flowers and elfin trees, brilliant in autumn, offers the intimate amid the vast.

In the Brooks Range, the natural world is sovereign. Man goes on its terms, acknowledging allegiance to the Earth. One reward is that sense of adventure, without which Robert Marshall maintained, life would be a dreary game. Gates of the Arctic is the evocative name given to a dramatic pair of mountains flanking the North Fork of the Koyukuk River by Marshall, a founder of the American wilderness system and an early explorer of the Brooks Range. The two peaks, Frigid Crags and Boreal Mountain, seem like massive gates opening into a cold region of mystery.

Scenes of grandeur are common here. In places, molten rocks have pushed through the backbone of the range to create such granite spires as the Arrigetch Peaks. Twenty miles to the west, at the head of the beautiful Reed River Valley, stands double-turreted Mount Igikpak, at 8,500 feet the highest summit in the central Brooks Range.

The spectacular peaks, like the valleys below them, were carved by the force of moving ice. Glaciers chiseled both the tilted rock mass of Cockedhat Mountain and the spire of Mount Doonerak, named by Marshall for an Eskimo supernatural being. Few glaciers remain in the park, for snowfall is no longer sufficient to form them.

In their rugged austerity, the park's precipitous peaks are stark counterpoints to wide-sweeping valleys, verdant and flowered in summer, bright with autumn coloration. In the spring, when winter's darkness and bitterest cold have passed, these valleys are natural routes for travel by dogsled or skis. By late June they become inviting avenues for hikers.

Creeks and rivers drain countless canyons, plateaus, and lakes to join larger streams, some bound north or west for the Beaufort and Chukchi seas and others south for the Yukon. Many of the park's waterways are among the finest float streams in Alaska — Noatak, Alatna, Killik, upper Koyukuk and Kobuk, and the John. They are generally clear, for they are not fed by glaciers. Helping to feed these rivers are several pristine lakes. Created by glaciers, they are found on both sides of the range, from Lake Selby in the forested Kobuk Valley to Kurupa Lake in the treeless north. Walker Lake, largest in the region, illustrates classic glacial formation and consequent ecologic development.

The parkland's broad scope is essential for perpetuation of its primitive character, its far-ranging wildlife, and the fragile veneer of vegetation — nourished by a thin mantle of frost-based soil. Thousands of migrating caribou sift through the mountain passes. The lichens upon which the caribou feed may take decades to grow an inch, so these animals must constantly migrate to conserve their own range. Twice each year the caribou respond to almost imperceptible forces that trigger their nomadic instincts — the length of the days, the texture of snowcrust. Calf survival depends on the precisely timed arrival of the pregnant females at Arctic Slope calving grounds just then bursting with nutritious cottongrass. The parkland

is also prime habitat for wolves, grizzlies, and Dall sheep. The howling chorus, the plate-size pawprint on river bar, the flecks of white on distant slope continually remind one of elusive life all around. Birds from Europe, South America, Asia, and tropic archipelagos congregate here to breed and nest in summer's rushing moments.

Thousands of years ago other explorers came to these mountains. The hints they have left us reveal that the caribou hunt has dominated human life here since the earliest occupations. For the Nunamiut Eskimos of Anaktuvuk Pass, the Kobuk Eskimos, and the northernmost Koyukon Indians the hunt continues. Their cultures are still rooted in traditional subsistence ways of life; their hunting and fishing places are respected within the parkland.

Gates of the Arctic possesses a general significance that embraces and transcends its particular elements, individually outstanding as they may be. That central meaning is the gaunt, haunting beauty of the Brooks Range and its tenuous life. It is an esthetic quality, a mood — qualities and moods, rather, for the region's character changes subtly valley to valley, north to south, and east to west. At first there may seem to be a sameness to the accordant summits, the scoured valleys, the tundra-dominated landscapes. But experience in the region reveals its varied aspects. The majestic sweep of the country around the Gates is far different from the goblin pinnacles around Mount Igikpak. The gentle, lichen-covered hills around the upper Kobuk contrast with the crags that rise above the John. The deep valley of the stately Reed, framed in spruce trees, presents a view far different from the stark sweep of the Killik River's arctic foothills.

The greatest resource of all is space — space for wandering, space for solitude and a sense of discovery. For 300 years Americans have benefitted from such space, with its opportunities to go forth to wilderness adventure. First beyond the Appalachians, then the Missouri and the Rockies, then to Alaska. This is the last

of it. Combined with neighboring Noatak, big, beautiful, beckoning wild landscapes stretch no farther under the United States flag. ∎

adapted from John Kauffmann

The view from the top gave us an excellent idea of the jagged country toward which we were heading. The main Brooks Range divide was entirely covered with snow. Close at hand, only about ten miles air line to the north, was a precipitous pair of mountains, one on each side of the North Fork. I bestowed the name of Gates of the Arctic on them, christening the east portal Boreal Mountain and the west portal Frigid Crags.

Three miles up the plunging creek we suddenly came upon a gorgeous lake, a mile and a half long and fresh as at creation. Great mountains rose directly from its shores and disappeared about 3,000 feet above the water into low-lying clouds. How far they jutted above the zone of visibility we could not even guess, but seeing the sweep of the mountains end in oblivion gave an impression of infinite heights beyond the experience of man. Nothing I had ever seen . . . had given me such a sense of immensity as this virgin lake lying in a great cleft in the surface of the earth with mountain slopes and waterfalls tumbling from beyond the limits of visibility. We walked up the right shore among bare rocks intermingled with meadows of bright lichen, while large flocks of ducks bobbed peacefully and unmindful of us on the water of the lake, and four loons were singing that rich, wild music which they have added to the beautiful melodies of earth. No sight or sound or smell or feeling even remotely hinted of men or their creations. It seemed as if time had dropped away a million years and we were back in a primordial world. It was like discovering an unpeopled universe where only the laws of nature held sway.

Robert Marshall[1]

16

quite another, and so the very steepness which added so much to the grandeur of the canyon made a descent to it with horses impossible. As we continued our side hill route grew rougher and rougher. We both scouted for ways down but without avail. After another mile we had to rest the horses and so we ate lunch. During this rest period Al found a snail in the dry bed of a receded glacier, a most surprising place. We saved it for Mozely & bored several trees and found the exceedingly slow growth anticipated.

A mile after resuming our journey our sidehill route became so extremely rough they did not dare take the horses a step further. We decided to strike for the summit of the hill on the side of which we were travelling. At this point we were probably 1,200 feet above the river and about 1,300 feet below the peaks. We reached the summit after nearly losing the horses several times in the soft underfooting left behind by the recently receded glacier.

The view from the top gave us an excellent idea of the jagged country toward which we were heading. The main Brooks Range divide was so high that it was entirely crowned with snow. Close at hand, only about 10 miles air line to the north, was the exceedingly precipitous east portal of the Gates to the Arctic, which I tentatively christened Oreal. The west portal I called the Frigid Crags. To the east and southeast also stretched range after range of uncalled mountains, less rugged than those to the north,

courtesy of the Bancroft Library, University of California, Berkeley, California 94720

I hope we will make no small decisions, but will act on a scale that befits the grandeur of this land.

Russell Train[2]

There is, to be sure, a kind of biotic riot in the summer outburst of color, scent, and sound . . . But always the season's opposite haunts you: what about the winter? What must that be like?

David Roberts[3]

We stopped for a late-morning rest. The sun was so strong, the air still so warm, that we took off our shirts to let them dry, and sat, bare-chested, feeling the soft breeze cool our skin. It did not seem possible that we were more than a hundred miles above the Arctic Circle.

"All this is a lie," Ray Bane said. "A beautiful lie. Winter is the truth about Alaska."

Joe McGinniss[4]

They were traveling steadily along now, a great mass of dark brown figures, bulls, cows, calves, yearlings, every combination of coloring, all bathed in the bright golden light of this Arctic night. The quiet, unmoving landscape I had scanned so carefully from the ridge before dinner had come alive. The rightful owners had returned.

This was the culmination of all the good things the river and the mountains had already shown us. Here was the living, moving, warm-blooded life of the Arctic.

Margaret Murie[5]

It was a spectacle like none other left on Earth now. It had power over the spirit. The power lay not only in what you saw — this slender column driving onward into wilderness. It lay also in what you knew. Arctic night and hunger coming. . . . Knowledge of danger and darkness and fear, built into their tissues by the centuries. Life and the cold Arctic before you for a moment in one silent sweep of land and moving animals.

Lois Crisler[6]

Two days ago, the morning sun emerged from behind the mountains shortly after noon, rode low along the southern crest for a brief half hour, then "set" behind the peaks to the south.

Yesterday, the full day's passage of the sun above the horizon lasted only ten minutes.

Today the sun has vanished.

At midday, its light from behind the far mountains is only a bright distant glow backlighting the horizon. Within our mountain-ringed world, the sky is clear but the light is gray, sunless. By two in the afternoon, the highest mountaintops to the north are crowned by sunset pinks — but there is no glimpse of a setting sun. . . .

All my knowledge, my data, my life experience with sun and warmth, with its absence and cold, has not equipped me to grasp this stark connectedness of earth and sun, as has this day while I watched for the sun to reappear and it did not.

The long night begins.

Billie Wright[7]

The insulation of the snow is what makes heat retention — and life — possible. The October freeze-up, therefore, in those weeks before much snow has fallen, is a bad time for the small animals that do not hibernate. Tundra voles foraging in October avoid exposure to the heat sink of the darkening sky. When they can they stick to the cover of rocks and hanging vegetation. For the voles, and for all arctic animals in winter, outer space dips closer to Earth. The infinite cold of an impartial firmament sucks the warmth from any body that is not deeply furred or feathered. For tundra voles, a view of the stars — so silent, large, and bright in arctic winter — is a premonition of death.

Kenneth Brower[8]

Goddammit, I like this country. I don't ever want to go out, only to visit my folks once before they die. But I'd just as leave die here as anywhere. I'd keep better.

A miner on the Koyukuk, quoted in Robert Marshall's Journal[9]

Adventure, whether physical or mental, implies breaking into unpenetrated ground, venturing beyond the boundary of normal aptitude, extending oneself to the limit of capacity, courageously facing peril. Life without the chance for such exertions would be for many persons a dreary game, scarcely bearable in its horrible banality. . . .

In a civilization which requires most lives to be passed amid inordinate dissonance, pressure and intrusion, the chance of retiring now and then to the quietude and privacy of sylvan haunts becomes for some people a psychic necessity. It is only the possibility of convalescing in the wilderness which saves them from being destroyed by the terrible neural tension of modern existence. . . .

Finally, it is well to reflect that the wilderness furnishes perhaps the best opportunity for pure esthetic enjoyment. This requires that beauty be observed as a unity, and that for the brief duration of any pure esthetic experience the cognition of the observed object must completely fill the spectator's cosmos. . . . In the wilderness, with its entire freedom from the manifestations of human will, that perfect objectivity which is essential for pure esthetic rapture can probably be achieved more readily than among any other forms of beauty.

Robert Marshall[10]

Here in the Brooks Range . . . tundra is . . . a primary life form. Making up this vast carpet of vegetation are low grasses, sedges, mosses, lichens and intertwined, diminutive bushes. The plants vary from place to place, depending upon exposure and drainage, and there are dry forms as well as wet, boggy tundra.

Boyd Norton[11]

Several willow stands along the river offer potential campsites particularly where the course of the river runs at a right angle to the alignment of the valley. One may camp on the west side of such stands gaining the maximum protection from the east wind. Sites conducive to long term camping are found in small willow lined draws along the sides of the valley. The Twelve Mile Creek draw on the northeast side of the valley appears to be an attractive campsite with excellent protection from the wind and an ample supply of large willows. These well protected draws in strategic locations undoubtedly drew human users since their earliest occupation of this area.

We stopped and set up camp at 2:30 pm in a small willow grove near the mouth of Twelve Mile Creek. Both we and the dogs are a bit tired from today's travel. Setting up camp, gathering dry willows, chopping and melting ice for water, preparing dogfood and feeding the dogs, cooking for ourselves, etc. takes three to four hours. Then harnesses have to be dried, repairs made to equipment, the day's notes written up, clothes dried, etc. By the time all this is done it's time to crawl into the sleeping bag and turn out the lamp.

Ascending Tupik Creek leads one to Angiaak Pass and thence to the headwaters of the Reed River. This passage has historically been utilized by the Kobuk River Eskimos in their subsistence exploitation of the upper Noatak region. This use is emphasized by the name given the Reed River by the Natives. Its Eskimo name literally means "The Going Home River."

Given the strategic significance of the Tupik Creek-Angiaak Pass route in the traditional subsistence activities of the Kobuk Eskimos, and the likelihood that it served as a major route between the upper Noatak and upper Kobuk River drainages for earlier inhabitants, an archeological survey might turn up some very interesting sites. Kobuk Eskimo tradition speaks of a group of Indians that once inhabited the upper Noatak Valley and of hostilities between the two cultural groups. The shelter from the wind and abundant willows at the mouth of the Tupik probably made it a popular campsite for aboriginal travelers making use of the nearby pass. . . . We cannot help but be overwhelmed with the sense of wilderness, but we are also aware that man has walked this land before the beginning of history. The confined valley roofed by the low overcast makes one feel as though he is in the ruined halls of an ancient civilization where only the ghosts of the past continue to reside.

Ray and Barbara Bane
Field notes from the upper Noatak
March, 1981

Mardy and I went up the valley, explored the shores of some little lakes. We came to a side-stream too deep to cross, so took a wide circular course back toward camp. On the way, we found nests of tree sparrows, always tucked into the moss on the ground, often in the base of a clump of dwarf birch. All were lined with soft white feathers of ptarmigan, and had one to five eggs. In my notes is the following:

"As I looked into these little hollows that were to be the future tree sparrow homes, I had the impression of looking into a dainty boudoir, so white and pure and clean, so appropriate a place for the birth of young birds."

As we roamed in this Arctic paradise during June and July, when this northland is benign, we became acquainted with the diverse manifestations of its life. The lichens on the cliffs and jumbled rocks, the mosses, the flowers blooming humbly among the tundra tussocks, all had a strong appeal.

Olaus Murie[12]

With a summer too short to complete a full life-cycle, almost all these plants are perennial. Many are xerophytes (adapted to long drought) with leathery leaves to minimize moisture losses. Low, cushion-like growth resists drying and wind abrasion, and also helps create a microclimate that may reach 40 degrees above air temperature. Shallow root systems utilize the soil's active layer above the permafrost. Roots of certain plants develop thermotropism (the ability to grow toward warmer portions of soil).

Robert Belous

From the saddle above the tributary valley we had a last look at the south slope of the Brooks Range. It was a vast country of rolling arctic moors and mild bare mountains, dappled by sunlight through cloud, and it seemed to slope away forever.

Kenneth Brower[13]

Willow Ptarmigan
East Main,
Feb. 15, 1914

field sketch by Olaus Murie courtesy of M. E. Murie

*To understand
the Earth . . .*

The Noatak is the largest mountain-ringed wilderness river basin in North America. It has a scope, a sweep as awesome and unforgettable as the desert or the Great Plains. There is variety as well — gaunt mountains and canyons, leagues of undulating, tundra-covered moraines, and, in its lower course, pond-spangled taiga and delta lowlands. Most important, the Noatak basin holds in trust a scientific repository. Here, rare Eurasian and North American life forms mingle in habitats sufficiently large, remote, and intact to give hope for their continued perpetuation in a rapidly changing world.

The Noatak is 450 miles long. It rises in part from the residual glaciers on 8,500-foot Mount Igikpak, its turreted summit the highest and most spectacular of central Brooks Range peaks. The river then courses through a deep U-shaped valley for the first 50 miles of its length. After leaving the confines of the Schwatka Mountains, the Noatak winds across a vast till plain. Long moraines follow the river, which occasionally cuts through them in bouldery rapids. So wide does the central valley become that the mountains ringing it — the Bairds on the south and, to the north, the DeLong Mountains forming the Arctic Divide — appear distant, small and blue. Ten rivers are tributary to the Noatak, as are nearly 40 named creeks, and the basin has countless lakes.

Midway down its course the Noatak enters its Grand Canyon, a scenic valley 70 miles long. Then it cuts for 6 miles between the sheer walls of Noatak Canyon, a true river gorge. Most of the upper basin is almost treeless tundra, with only a few willows and balsam poplars along the waterways. Near the river's great bend from the mountains toward the sea, however, scattered stands of spruce mark the northwesternmost reach of the boreal forest in North America. As the river turns and courses southward, the forest thickens and the river divides into many channels through a wide valley where myriad ponds and sloughs provide ideal habitat for whistling swans and other waterfowl.

In this area 70 miles from the sea the Noatak passes the only settlement in its entire basin, Noatak village, population about 300. Then the current slackens, although the river pierces one more chain of uplands, the Igichuk Hills, through lower Noatak Canyon before spreading through a delta to empty into Kotzebue Sound.

The *Nuatakmiit,* the people of the Noatak, and their neighbors from surrounding areas continue to use the Noatak drainage for hunting, fishing, and travel through the passes that connect arctic and subarctic Alaska. Before them, Early Man and ancestral Eskimos traversed the same pathways, marked still earlier by the caribou. These millennia of human use left only scattered remains of camps and caches lost in space. For others the Noatak has been a mystery, only partially unveiled by infrequent explorations beginning in the 1880s. Recent expeditions, beset by problems of arctic logistics and lack of time, have only sampled the trove that awaits scientists here. They suspect that they are missing much, and they want to come back. Is the Noatak a sparer, arctic version of Africa's Serengeti Plain? After all, two-thirds of the largest caribou herd in America pours through Howard and other passes and across the valley twice each year en route between Arctic Slope calving grounds and wintering areas to the south. And the Noatak seems to be essential habitat for the barren-ground grizzly. It is wolf and wolverine country as well. Dall sheep inhabit its mountains. Chum salmon and Arctic char ascend its rivers.

What about the Noatak's use by waterfowl and by Asian bird species? The endangered peregrine falcon has been sighted. Also a curlew, which could have been an Eskimo curlew, feared to be extinct. What about vegetation in this meeting ground of tundra and taiga, of arctic and subarctic biomes? Could the Noatak also be a botanical Shangri-la?

The 1974 designation of the Noatak region as an international biosphere reserve under the UNESCO

Man and Biosphere Program signals its world significance and the chance to answer these questions. The purpose of such reserves was stated by Christian A. Herter, Jr., of the Department of State:

> It is our intention . . . to use these areas as reservoirs for preserving wild plants and animals to assure that the genetic material they represent will not be lost. This material is valuable not only for the sake of preservation itself for future generations to know, but also for conserving natural genetic pools which may be used to revitalize or improve the productivity of plants and animals upon which man's existence depends. . . . Biosphere reserves will be experimental areas where studies are conducted of living, changing plant and animal systems, how they relate to each other, and how man's activities offset and are affected by them.

And so the Noatak waits upon the stewardship and studies that will decide its destiny. Wide and bare but with a subtlety of light and space and landforms that creates the austere delicate beauty of northern Alaska, it seems an empty place. Yet it is filled with hardy but tenuous life existing in a complex of sensitive interfacings and comminglings. The Noatak is an environment about which we need to learn far, far more than the little we now surmise. Its wilderness offers knowledge: how to understand the Earth, utilize it gently, and so survive. ∎

adapted from John Kauffmann

Our studies of the Noatak watershed in the summer of 1973 found the region a fascinating transition zone and migration route for plants and animals between subarctic and arctic environments, between tundra (treeless plains) and taiga (subarctic coniferous forests), without peer except perhaps in eastern Siberia in its variety of terrain and habitat.

Except for coastal formations, virtually every type of arctic habitat is found somewhere in the Noatak

drainage, usually with a full complement of circumpolar life. With 413 species of vascular plants counted during that one summer of study and the full roster of species in the area expected to be in the neighborhood of 500, the Noatak's flora is as large as that of the entire Alaskan Arctic Slope and larger than the flora of the whole Canadian arctic archipelago. Indeed, the Noatak may have the finest array of flora anywhere in the far north. Close to the region where Asia and America were once joined, the Noatak is also a prime location for studying a rich biota focused there by convergent influences from most of the major mountain systems of the world.

Archeology is there as well, close beneath the tundra. Evidence indicates that the Noatak basin may have been occupied by man as long ago as 10,000 years. Perhaps the region holds clues to man's entry into the New World across the Bering Land Bridge. The 1973 studies provided further evidence of an inland wintertime settlement of the Ipiutak culture which utilized the region about 2,000 years ago. Other archeological finds revealed human use of the upper Noatak at a time 4,000 to 5,000 years ago when some scholars had assumed glaciers still held sway.

adapted from Steve Young[1]

The size of the Noatak basin is such that it is a true wilderness rather than an enclave of wild country surrounded by civilization on all sides. In terms of the scope and complexities of the environment, there is certainly no situation left in the 'lower 48' that is remotely comparable. We feel that the Noatak valley and the surrounding countryside afford one of the last opportunities in the United States, or for that matter the entire world, to set aside for the future a wilderness of such size, variability and complexity that it functions as a complete ecosystem. If this opportunity is not seized upon, it will never occur again.

Steve Young[2]

Excerpts from the narrative of exploration of the Noatak River in 1885, by S. B. McLenegan, engineer, U.S. Revenue Steamer, Corwin.

The services of a native guide could not be obtained, and, although the undertaking was a desperate venture, I determined to go without native assistance of any kind, and felt that [Seaman Nelson and I] must depend wholly upon ourselves for the success of the undertaking.... The moment of our final parting had now come, and, under the circumstance, knowing nothing of the dangers before us, it was not a pleasant one. With the appearance of cheerfulness, however, we bade them farewell, and resolutely turned the canoe towards the north.

The rain of the day continued throughout the night, and the following morning brought no change with it. Notwithstanding the dreary prospect, we resumed our journey, hoping to find a better condition of affairs further along. Contrary to my expectations, the nature of our work seemed more hopeless than before; the current seemed to increase in strength every mile of our journey, and before we had proceeded very far above the camp we were obliged to abandon the paddles and place ourselves in the tracking harness.

We had now gained one of the most desolate sections of country imaginable; in gazing over the portion already traveled nothing met the eye save an unbroken stretch of flats, unrelieved by forests or hills.... The sense of utter desolation and loneliness which took possession of the mind was indeed difficult to dispel.... No trace of human habitations could be found, and even the hardy waterfowl seemed to have foresaken the region, leaving nothing to remind us of the great and busy world thousands of miles below.

Shortly after noon we entered the Grand Canyons of the Noatak, a section about three miles in length, and by far the most interesting portion we had yet seen. Here the perpendicular walls rose hundreds of feet on either side, seldom offering a foothold along the bases, while the tops frequently overhung the river and seemed to threaten momentarily to topple over and crush us beneath their ponderous weight. As the river from above enters the canyons it plunges forward with an almost irresistible force.

One of the most noticeable features developed during the day was the entire absence of timber of any description; no driftwood could be found along the banks, and it was very evident that we had passed the timber limit and would soon reach the table-lands of the interior, if my theory in regard to the character of that region proved correct.

The stream again pursued a very tortuous course, winding in and around the mountains, through deep canyons and gorges, where, in spite of the wretched weather, we could not fail to admire the grandeur of the scenery. In the mean time the fresh breeze of morning had increased into a gale which fairly whistled through the chasms, and hoisting our sail, we were driven rapidly forward, notwithstanding the opposing current in the river. The work now became exciting in the extreme. . . . Imbued with a spirit of boldness bordering on recklessness, the canoe was driven before the gale.

Directly above here the river, by a sharp turn, leaves the mountains and enters upon a country of an entirely different character. Indeed, this sudden transformation of scene is one of the most peculiar and striking features of the Noatak River region.

As we entered upon this last section I cannot convey an idea of the picture which met our view. Behind us the dark wall of mountains through which we had just passed towered upward until their summits were lost in the clouds, and seemed like an impassable barrier, shutting us off from the outside world. Before us lay the level plains of the interior, stretching away in the distance, unrelieved by a single object upon which the eye could rest with any feeling of pleasure.

A fresh breeze sprang up, and as usual, we made sail in order to lighten our labor. Proceeding in this manner for a mile or more we reached a rapid portion of the river, which I determined, if possible, to sail through, hoping to save the cold bath which would otherwise be involved, for the tracking line could not be used in passing it. By dint of hard work we had gotten about half way through when the bidarka fouled with a sunken rock. Before the calamity could be averted the canoe had whirled broadside to the current and capsized. Fortunately the water was not deep, and so soon as our senses were recovered we righted the craft and put into the bank. A survey of the damage revealed only a thorough wetting, and our next impulse was to indulge in a hearty laugh, even though there was nothing particularly ludicrous in the situation. The canoe had partly filled with water, by which everything was more or less damaged. The only serious loss was that of our footgear, which, by some unaccountable means, had disappeared in the excitement of the moment. Otherwise than an icy bath, however, and the loss mentioned, we experienced no particular hardship. . . . Indeed, the difficulties encountered only seemed to awaken the stubborn elements of our natures, and with a determination not to be baffled, we prepared ourselves to meet anything short of utter annihilation.

Late in the afternoon we found on the left bank what appeared to be a grave, and, prompted by curiosity, I determined to halt and examine it. Upon gaining the spot we discovered that it was a well-disguised cache, containing a large quantity of skins, native clothing, boots, and a general assortment of native possessions, together with a sledging outfit. The significance of these caches now became evident; the extreme difficulty attending the navigation above this point made it clear that the natives, on returning from the coast, abandoned the river here and completed their journey on sledges.

We had now gone beyond the head of canoe navigation and had reached, practically speaking, the headwaters of the river. The vast number of lakes which covered the face of the country, all of which were drained by the river, made it evident that it could not be traced to one source. Above us the Noatak divided into several branches, and as none were navigable, further progress was manifestly impossible. Every effort had been made to accomplish the object of the expedition, and now that we had achieved all that lay in our power, I determined to retreat without delay.

Late in the evening we gained the rapids above the canyons, and, with a common impulse, grasped the paddles for the coming struggle. Finally, after rounding a sharp turn, the canyons suddenly loomed up ahead, the lofty walls of which towered hundreds of feet above us. Swiftly we were drawn in by the rushing waters and soon gained the gloomy depths of the gorge. Every faculty was now on the alert, for the dangers seemed to multiply as we advanced.

About 2 o'clock we entered the "home stretch" of the river and eagerly strained our eyes to catch the first glimpse of the sea. In the distance, on the opposite shore of the inlet, the clear-cut headlands stood out in bold relief against the evening sky. The feelings of joy and relief which rose within us found no room for expression, and the prospect of a speedy termination of our journey, after the many hardships of the summer, was indeed cheering.

S. B. McLenegan

I'm paddling alone, while Gladys sleeps. We float quietly through the landscape. My ears are attuned to the whisper of water dripping off the paddle. A loon cries from afar. . . . This is intimate country — old, and softened by time. Looking across the vastness, I can visualize the mammoths and bisons of old, browsing in the grassland steppes while most of North America lay ice-covered, dormant. In every direction I see distant mountains beyond the miles of tussocky tundra, grassy swales, thaw ponds, lakes, and creeks. Sun sweeps across the river as it shines through a break in the clouds. It is warm for a few moments, then immediately the shadows sweep upriver and it is chill again.

The wind is now blowing upriver and paddling becomes more difficult. My strokes mostly serve to keep the bow of the raft facing downstream. The water level has risen more than a foot since yesterday and flows swiftly in muddied intensity. The raft reels; I feel we are just another piece of debris flowing with the current.

Gladys awakens, remarking on the chill in the air. She joins me paddling and we fall into a rhythm of stroking, as the wind increases and droplets sound that familiar thud on the rubber raft. Suddenly, a wall of rain sweeps over us; paddling becomes more than steering; we are now fighting just to stay on the river. Each meander places us in yet a different position with respect to the wind and we are invariably either blown up on the shore or blown back upriver — but never is the wind to our advantage. Each stroke becomes a shoulder-socket wrenching pull, and as the squall moves in full force, the rain completely envelopes us.

We continue our stroking rhythm, ignoring fatigue. In all its intensity, it is wonderful to be a part of this storm. At Okak Bend, I look up on a tundra slope to see several caribou quietly grazing. They raise their heads a moment in observation, then return to eating. Gulls cavort overhead, unmindful of the wind and rain. A few scaup beat by. But mostly, we're on our own — two women on the Noatak, the tundra and mountains all around, the great sky overhead.

Karen Jettmar

*At the edge
of the forest . . .*

This enclosed valley provides settings of great beauty and variety for its wealth of historical and continuing cultural associations. The Kobuk River, rising on the south flank of the Brooks Range, is usually a clear and placid stream of deep meanders and changing scenes. Its major tributary within the park, the Salmon, descends in turbulence from the Baird Mountains, then widens and collects in deep pools of extraordinary blue-green hue.

The Great Kobuk Sand Dunes form the largest active dune field in arctic North America. Dunes attain a height of 100 feet as they crest under pressure from the valley's prevailing easterly winds. The great volume of sand derives from glacial drift and outwash originating in the Baird and Schwatka mountains to the north. Sand forms display a full spectrum from U-shaped and concave dunes to the crescent-shaped barchan dunes of the Earth's driest regions. Samplings of peat bog below the sand show the age of the dunes to be greater than 33,000 years.

Surrounding the dunes — in a broad transition zone between taiga forest and arctic tundra — a blend of the two has produced an inviting parklike landscape of open birch and spruce stands on a springy carpet of caribou lichen. Across the lowlands, relict outcrops of sage brush and grass give clues to the long sweep of natural and human history that has forged a bond between the two in this quiet valley.

Arctic and subarctic overlap in Kobuk Valley's mountain-rimmed basin. Rivers, forests, and tundra blend in a mosaic that is neighbored by arctic seas and estuaries. In ancient times this basin — surrounded by glaciers but unglaciated itself — formed a part of a cold and dry arctic steppeland occupied by grazing animals, including horses, antelopes, bison, and mammoths. Man entered this country practicing hunting skills learned on the Siberian steppes whence he came. This new hunting territory was then an extension of Siberia. Beringia — that broad geographic region comprising the Bering Land Bridge and its hinterlands — pulsed with migrations of plants and animals between Asia and America.

Biologically dynamic and varied then, the region remains so today. It is a place of shifting boundaries between the plants and animals of tundra and forest, of highlands and lowlands, of maritime and interior. It is even more complex than that. This meeting place of today's geographies and climates also has depth in time. Preserved in the unglaciated Kobuk basin are plant species that antedate the last glaciation. Though interwoven with modern flora, they present the impression of that ancient steppe.

In such a varied place, human hunters and gatherers capitalize on multiples of prey and plant species. But they must be ever alert to the dynamics of change in such a boundary land. They must flex with the changes — of climate, vegetation, and animals. In fact, Kobuk Valley is a classic cultural landscape that illustrates man's flexibility — horizontally across each era's environment, vertically through time.

Along the gently flowing Kobuk, archeological sites give clues to the cultural adaptations that allowed the people of the valley to keep pace with their changing world. For example, studies of ancient pollens show that valley vegetation changed from steppe tundra to shrub tundra about 9,000 years ago. This must have affected the kinds and distribution of animals available to human hunters. Is it mere coincidence that they shifted from use of heavy stone tools for butchering and skinning to delicate flaked implements? In Siberia, where the archeological record is clearer, it has been confirmed that a similar tool change marked the replacement of large Ice Age mammals with boreal species of more modern times.

The interplay continues between archeologists and their counterparts in biology, the paleoecologists. One of these, Charles Schweger, has shown that distribution of alder shrubs reached a maximum in the Kobuk Valley 4,500 years ago. Caribou do not relish alder.

Archeologist Douglas Anderson pondered the meaning of this: If caribou — the mainstay of interior arctic hunters — avoided the valley, what happened to the hunters? From that question flow others: Would the hunters have changed their orientation to other resources in the valley, possibly to a greater dependence on salmon? Would they have moved north of the mountains to better caribou range? Or might they have gone to the coast and become seal hunters for a few centuries until the alder thinned out and the caribou came back?

These are the sorts of puzzles that make arctic archeology interesting. And the Kobuk Valley may have the answers. At a river bend and caribou crossing known as Onion Portage, archeological investigations begun in 1940 by J. Louis Giddings have uncovered layers of hearths, tools, and other artifacts that trace human occupation back at least 12,500 years, through seven distinct cultural horizons. A few miles downriver, at *Ahteut,* scores of housepits and associated artifacts help define the Arctic Woodland Culture of 700 years ago, from which today's Kobuk Valley people descended.

The caribou and the salmon continue their migrations and the *Kuuvangmiit,* people of the Kobuk, continue to harvest them and adapt to a changing world. This park helps to perpetuate the environment in which cultural choices can be made. The Eskimo people have faced change and the need for choice many times before. They have been here a long time. ■

Our small wall tent formed a self-contained cell of warmth in the vast supercooled arctic wilderness. Outside the thin canvas walls the temperature was −43°F. and would fall even further before morning. The sheet metal camp stove glowed a dull red as it hungrily consumed sticks of spruce and alder. The tent was dimly lit by a crude lamp fashioned from tin which held a long wick that absorbed and burned seal oil. Joe

Sun, a 74 year old Kobuk River Eskimo, sat on a caribou skin mat near the stove tending the primitive lamp. The flame sent shadows flitting across his craggy, leather-colored face. His soft voice blended with the subdued surroundings as he told the old stories and cultural history of his people. He spoke of the exploits of cultural heroes, of the battles with the Iyugmiut, a fierce tribe of Indians that once lived in the mountains, of how he and other men would walk the high country of the Brooks Range seeking meat and skins, and how they dared turbulent streams on small rafts to return home. As he talked he described the land, naming lakes, streams, mountains, passes, and other features as though he was describing pictures set before him. Immersed in the flow of his words and the mood of our setting I could literally feel myself slipping back through time to a world unaffected by modern technology and mega-

culture. I briefly found myself looking at the world through the eyes of an ancient people.

Ray Bane

Beyond question fur clothing is the only kind suitable for Arctic wear, and it should conform in material and cut to that worn by the natives. The members of the expedition wore deerskin [caribou] coats with hoods (parkies), deerskin trousers, deerskin boots and deerskin socks, over underclothing of flannel. The parkies are shaped like a shirt with a hole in the neck just large enough to admit the head; around the back of the hole the hood is sewed. They are double, the inner skin being light with the fur turned towards the body, while the outer skin is of the heaviest with the hair turned out.

Lt. George M. Stoney, 1885

[The men] tried to get new barks for the canoes and boats. The old barks were taken off and new ones put on. . . . The boats were sewn with willow roots. Willow and tree roots were used as thread, and spruce gum was used for plugging up the seams. We did not have the corking material. We melted the gum, using birch bark as a pot or container. We melted the gum slowly in a campfire. We used the tree gum on the seams after putting on new barks. We always put a new bark cover on the kayak before the salmon fishing. . . .

After we fixed the boats, the fish came. We worked really hard to catch salmon. We caught so many that sometimes we didn't have the time to finish them all. Sometimes they caught sheefish, too. The men went to the headwaters of the river and then up into the mountains. They went up to hunt mountain sheep, and if they found caribou, they would hunt them too, to get the skins for clothing. They also hunted marmot for their bedding. After the men left, the women that stayed behind worked on catching a lot of fish. . . .

We ate fresh fish and ducks. We also ate rhubarb and sourdock which we mixed with our food. Sometimes we had no seal oil, but we had oil from the marmot, and also the fish oil we made at Avaragaaniq. That was the way we lived and that was how I was raised with my grandparents.

Jenny Jackson, born in
Kobuk Village about 1893[1]

Our elders . . . have what is most important to them, the knowledge of their environment. Their laws might not be written, but they are given in another sense. The taboos, superstitions that have been passed on, work as sufficiently as the laws that are written in books for average society. Even their knowledge of weather, which is vital to the people. One has to know the conditions of the weather before going out hunting or fishing. Who knows, you may never see him again.

Louie Commack
(Aquppak)

For Native Alaskans, the landscape is comprised of myriad special or unique places, which are considered different from all other places in the known world. The uniqueness of these places derives not only from their particular resource potentials or economic values, but also from their association with the oral history or traditions of the people in question. These associations are completely invisible and inaccessible to an outsider, existing only in the minds of the people who know them. . . .

I think about this constantly when I explore new places in the south forty-eight, wondering what lost meanings there were, what kind of sacredness or sorcery or historical richness I am moving amidst without knowing it. In my mind, it seems that a large measure of that land has been lost — even if the places remain intact and unaltered, much of their deepest meaning in human terms has vanished.

Richard Nelson

[By the late 1940s] . . . we knew a good deal about the present natives of the river as well as their ancestors who had dwelt along its shores for the past seven hundred years. All seemed to have lived well, comfortable in their warm, underground houses. While the upper river people depended upon goods that utilized products of the luxurious birch and spruce forests, and, in later years, specialized in jade work, there were obvious similarities between the upper river sites and those of its mouth at Kotzebue. Not all these could be easily tied in with the coastal Eskimo pattern found on islands and peninsular points. There seemed a remarkable interdependence between the people not only of one culture period but of all who lived within the valley of the Kobuk, and I pondered much about this.

Old Eskimos pointed out that formerly men were always on the move. While women fished for salmon during the summer, husbands and sons roamed the high mountains amassing pelts for winter clothing, bedding, and tents. In autumn, whole families traveled together to the lakes and slopes where caribou habitually crossed, then returned, later in the fall, to rebuild or refurbish their winter houses. Home, for

these people, was not a single spot but an area within which they moved during the course of a year. Some few men of the upper Kobuk attended the trading fair at Kotzebue in late summer, distributing, upon their return, goods from the coast — seal oil, whaleskin, amber, and metal goods. Then in midwinter most of the river people, including those of Kotzebue, traveled some distance for an annual festival of trading and gift-giving.

Though it seemed likely that the language spoken earlier was Eskimo, as it is today, I could not discount the strong emphasis on inland products and the resemblances of many practices to those of neighboring Athapaskan Indians. Present and recent people of the river might be called Eskimos because of their language, yet their culture had been different enough to warrant their not being categorized by so fixed a name. Instead, thinking of all the older and continuing cultures of the river, varied as they were in content and based upon the contiguity of high mountains, lakes, inland forests, food-giving rivers, and a branch of the sea, I called these people the "Arctic Woodlanders." We had found many of their obvious sites, yet these must have only scratched the surface, for it was hard to conceive of any time since the glaciers when people living anywhere in the region of Bering Strait would not have found and exploited the Kobuk or neighboring forested streams.

Pegliruk, a Kobuk man in his seventies who had talked to me in 1940, told of life as he remembered it at the caribou crossings before white men came to the river. The men and older boys of a group customarily spent the summer away from their women hunting in the high mountains for the pelts of sheep and young caribou. Returning to their homes in early fall when the women were just drying the last salmon of the season, the men joined their womenfolk and began a journey up the river by boat to their customary rendezvous with other families at a caribou crossing. . . .

Once established in their new camp at the caribou crossing, the men built or repaired diverting fences to lead the caribou down slopes and into the water where they might be slaughtered with spears from one-man bark canoes. As soon as the animals began to appear, men, women, and children all took part, urging the caribou along until they plunged into the stream where the spearsmen waited. I could visualize the brown-gray herds pouring rhythmically over the bare slopes between the mouth of Jade Creek and Onion Portage, the splashing of paddles in the boats, the plunging of spears and knives into the demoralized swimmers, the spurts of blood mingling with the rush of the blue Kobuk water, and the dead and dying animals, held afloat by their buoyant coats, drifting with the current to the gravel beach at Onion Portage.

J. Louis Giddings[2]

Somewhat incredulous, I sank a limited test cut and found to my elation that there was no limit to the neatly stacked layering of old surfaces. Furthermore, the differences in nature and style of the flinty material in one after another of these charcoal-bearing layers showed that they were not simply the occupation zones of closely successive visitors. Rather, these strata suggested that unconnected peoples of the past, each with a distinctive flintworking technology, had lived on these various levels at the time they formed.

J. Louis Giddings
1961 field season[3]

We exposed the old surfaces in six-foot squares, one at a time, finding a sterile layer of yellowish sandy loam separating the Old Hearth band from Band 4. Then in the top layer of Band 4 we began to uncover a fireplace . . . . As we did so, a thin sliver of red jasper stood out above all else, and I saw with an excited glance that it was a burin spall, one of those minute implements used by Denbigh people . . . . Next came

from J. Louis Giddings, *Ancient Men of the Arctic*, Alfred A. Knopf, New York, 1977 raw flakes, and soon, a microblade . . . .

Other objects soon turned up, identical in every respect to artifacts and flakes of the Denbigh Flint complex, and together they announced, as if given voice, that Denbigh people, formerly known to have lived at the forest edge where trees meet tundra or bare mountain slopes, had also camped, here at Onion Portage, deep within the woods. . . .

If the Denbigh people at Onion Portage were contemporary with those on the coast, these layers of former ground surfaces had been camped on at least four or five thousand years ago.

I decided to excavate the older layers myself. . . . What, if any, culture would I find deeper than Denbigh; and was there no limit to the depth of the site? The trowelling seemed painfully slow as I dug ever deeper. Would there, perhaps, be spearheads of the Early Man types of the Great Plains? What chance was there that a notched point like those of Palisades II at Cape Krusenstern might show up to support my proposed dating of that site and give proof to my colleagues that the culture of Palisades II was older than Denbigh?

My trowel now led me deeper . . . . I was quite hidden from the view of those digging in other areas nearby. . . . With a shout to my fellow workers, I picked up from one of the upper layers of Band 6, a side-notched point, the first of many subsequently found . . . . Here was proof, from ancient layers deep in stratigraphy, that notched points elsewhere so rare in the Arctic were indeed old, and this at once strongly fortified my belief that the notched points found at the Palisades site back beyond all the beach ridges were of equally great age . . . . Had we, in the two sites, evidence of a group of people heretofore unknown?

J. Louis Giddings
1963 field season[4]

Like so many present-day land forms, the dunes date back to Pleistocene times when mountain glaciers were active in the Brooks Range. Broad, braided rivers carried abundant outwash material, and strong winds swept the sands and silts away to form the great dune fields. Disappearance of the glaciers eliminated the source of new material for the dunes, and the ridges of sand were gradually overgrown by vegetation, and became stable.

What is fascinating about the Great Kobuk Sand Dunes, and a smaller group a few miles to the east, is that they alone have resisted revegetation through the centuries. How do they differ from the much larger tracts of dead dunes nearby?

The answer lies in a particular combination of winds and topography. The east wind, clearly, is responsible for the main motion of the dunes. Steep, spectacular slopes face Kavet Creek along the western margin of the field, and at least one old stream bed shows that the creek has been overwhelmed by sand and forced westward; . . .

But if the east wind moves the sands, the north wind maintains them. It is no accident that the dunes lie against the foot of the mountains, for if that wall of rock were not there, the north wind would have carried the sands off to the south centuries ago. Lobes of sand lap at the slopes, as if the wind had lifted the grains upward until it could carry them no higher. The same winds desiccate and sandblast any seedling that manages to take root on the porous, sun-baked surface of the deep, well-drained sands; under such conditions, revegetation is impossible.

So the landscape is alive and changing as the sands inch slowly westward, and overwhelm even mature spruce trees. But hardy pioneering plants relentlessly colonize the quieter margins of the dunes, and the streams carry away a bit more sediment every year. Without a source of new sand, these dunes too must eventually die, and remain an undistinguished, sparsely forested hillside until the climate changes once again.

Ole Wik[5]

The Congress finds and declares that —
. . . the continuation of the opportunity for subsistence uses by rural residents of Alaska, including both Natives and non-Natives, on the public lands . . . is essential to Native physical, economic, traditional, and cultural existence and to non-Native physical, economic, traditional, and social existence.

Alaska Lands Act of 1980

✳

I have learned a great deal from the elders . . . . Although old people have traveled miles and labored hours for their food, the looks on their faces when talking about the past life proves how much life has meant to them . . . we still have those people to show us how to fish and hunt, and tell us about our culture if we are only willing to listen.

Louie Commack (Aquppak)

✳

Maybe Alaska isn't a place for words, but for sensations and feelings and thoughts that come together around the land, the people, and the animals who live together here. Alaskans express themselves best by responding actively and directly to the land.

Joseph Meeker[6]

✳

National parks must not serve as a means for displacing the members of traditional societies who have always cared for the land and its biota. Nor can national parks survive as islands surrounded by hostile people who have lost the land that was once their home.

Raymond Dasmann

CAPE KRUSENSTERN NATIONAL MONUMENT

*Along the
sea edge . . .*

The ancient beach ridges of Cape Krusenstern preserve an unbroken chronicle of every major phase of Eskimo prehistory. Behind the oldest beach ridges rise limestone palisades containing artifacts left by still earlier people, pre-Eskimo hunters who lived here before the beach ridges existed. The cape's archeological wealth — spread horizontally from today's shoreline across the miles of earlier shores — matches the compact vertical stratigraphy of human occupation at Onion Portage on the Kobuk River. Together, the two sites provide the benchmarks of arctic archeology.

Recent geological discoveries add more ties between Cape Krusenstern and its neighboring regions. The ancestral Noatak River once slanted westward to enter the sea a few miles north of Cape Krusenstern. During past ice ages the river corridor gave outlet to a great glacier bisecting the western end of the Brooks Range. The windy stretch of tussock tundra along the old glacier bed had long served as a trail for Eskimo seal hunters on their way from Noatak to coastal camps in spring. But recently, detailed inspection of aerial photos revealed an odd-shaped mound about 100 yards long. Ground tests showed it to be an esker, a molded formation of gravel created by a river inside a glacier. Since this place escaped the most recent glaciation during the Wisconsin period, some 20,000 years ago, the esker was verified to date back to the Illinoian period, some 200,000 years ago. It is the only one of this age ever found in Alaska.

This discovery helped to clarify the geological background for human history at Cape Krusenstern. For the seaward face of the old Illinoian glacier bed forms a major source of the beach gravel shuttled by wave action down to the cape. Once accumulated in offshore reservoirs, the gravel awaits the intervals every 50 to 75 years when south and southwesterly storms drive the gravel high and dry to form new beach fronts. Thus have the mountains been moved to the sea to form beaches for seal hunters' camps. The pebble tossed into the sea by today's Eskimo child may have come from the slopes of Mount Igikpak at the Noatak River's source.

The beach-building process at Cape Krusenstern continues today as it has for the past 5,000 years. In its day, each of the cape's 114 distinct beach ridges was the ocean front and campsite for early Eskimo hunters. Each ridge forms a repository for the tools, pottery, hearths, and artwork of its period, like pages of a book of human survival and cultural evolution in the Arctic.

Cape Krusenstern beautifully illustrates the continuing harmonies between environmental forces and opportunistic Eskimo subsisters. A good example is the fish-harvest location at *Anyiakk.* As the sole outlet for the Krusenstern Lagoon, *Anyiakk* becomes an immense fish trap each fall when wind and wave action block the outflow with beach gravel. Thousands of pounds of whitefish teem just behind the barrier in search of a way out to the sea. A shallow trench, or *kargisaak,* is dug in the gravel. The low flow of water is just enough to get the whitefish swarming through the bogus outlet. The fish wind up flopping high and dry as the water quickly seeps into the gravel before reaching the sea. Without hook, line, or net the trick has worked for generations.

Cape Krusenstern signifies the long chronology of man's survival at the outer edge of human habitat. Walking from back beach ridges where the now-distant ocean once lapped, one senses the ghosts of long-vanished hunters on their journey to the present: the Denbigh Flint people, the very first Eskimos; Old Whaling spearmen whose culture is strangely disassociated from those that preceded and followed it; the Choris and Norton people and their utilitarian artwork and practical tools; the emergence at about the time of Christ of the Ipiutak Eskimos, mystical artisans as well as hunters; and the wide-ranging people of the Western Thule period, who carried Eskimo language and lifeway as far east as Greenland.

As in no other single location, the cultural

landscape leads to a shoreline where the spring tent-camps of Eskimo seal hunters still luff in the arctic breeze as they have for thousands of years. Along the cape's outermost beach the chronicle is still being written, and hard-won techniques for survival acknowledge a debt to the people of the beaches of the past. The sounds of Eskimo voices still blend with the whisper of surf and shifting gravel as the next beach ridge is made ready.

adapted from Robert Belous

Often as I walked back across the many ridges at Cape Krusenstern I speculated about the people who had lived in this particular area. Their summers, like this, would have been cold at best, and the winters formidable. Since earliest times they would have

occupied themselves mainly with the quest for food, giving attention too, of course, to the essentials of keeping warm: adequate shelter and clothing. The procurement of food, for us, was little more difficult than a trip to the store at Kotzebue for canned meats, dry milk, or beans; but early dwellers on the oceanfront at Cape Krusenstern were entirely dependent on their success at trapping, snaring, shooting, harpooning, or netting whatever was available to fill their caches or food racks — unendingly, season after season. While food would have been their primary concern, ceremonial gatherings or periods of recreation must have given occasional pleasant changes. And from all of the people who lived on these beach ridges, sharing similar problems and hardships, there emerged through the centuries the Eskimo of today: a careful, watchful, fun-filled individual — crafty, brave, and enduring.

That night in camp . . . I sketched for the students of our group the history of Thule culture . . . [and] the daring way its people hunted whales and moved freely over ice floes and polar lands — lands that long ago became the base across the whole American Arctic coast for the Eskimos as we know them today.

The greatly skilled and meticulous art and technology of Ipiutak . . . are not easily associated with a highly nomadic people. Arrowheads were made of cylinders of ivory sharpened at the ends and fitted with either thin, triangular end blades or inset, semilunar blades of flinty material. Some of these delicate bifaces showed diagonal flaking on both faces. The manner of insetting side blades both in these small weapons and in knives and elaborate swords departed from any Eskimo patterns then known but conformed to Mesolithic and Neolithic ways of hafting blades in Siberia and other parts of the Old World.

from Louis J. Giddings, *Ancient Men of the Arctic*, Alfred A. Knopf, New York, 1977

Kneeling and carefully lifting patches of moss, we freed an area wide enough to give more details. A large number of pieces showed that one large cooking pot of this check-stamped ware had been broken and discarded by some ancient campers. . . .

Pottery of this type was typical of Norton culture which we knew to be older than Ipiutak. Why the art of making and using pottery was known by Norton people, and before them, Choris people of three thousand years ago, but was bypassed by Ipiutakers, only to be taken up again by more recent people, is still one of the unfathomables of Arctic archeology.

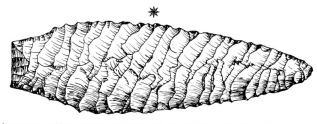

from Louis J. Giddings, *Ancient Men of the Arctic*, Alfred A. Knopf, New York, 1977

We had hardly begun to speculate on what these proofs of whaling in so early a site would mean to archeological theory when a large bifaced lance blade turned up. This was of chalcedony, with parallel edges and a straight base, but though over eight inches long it measured less than two inches wide. My first thought was that it was no Arctic specimen but one transplanted from Neolithic sites of North Europe or Egypt. This one, again, suggested no other implement of flint in the region, yet its shape and size were closely like the blades of polished slate used by recent Eskimos for killing and flensing whales.

Unlike all the other cultures in western Alaska, from that of present-day Eskimos to Choris, to the much

earlier Denbigh Flint culture, the Old Whaling culture showed no strong signs of continuity. The Denbigh people of 3000 B.C. had handed down certain traits to the Choris people of 1000 B.C. and these traits could be seen again in the more recent Norton and, especially, Ipiutak cultures. Why, then, did the Old Whalers of 1800 B.C. have no ties with their successors or their predecessors on this series of beach ridges at Cape Krusenstern?

. . . We found it hard to understand where the Old Whalers had come from and how they had broken the chain of events on the beaches at Cape Krusenstern. To the present day we can only speak of the Old Whaling culture as one might of a strange plant that suddenly appeared in his garden and then, after becoming firmly rooted and strong, disappeared one day without a trace.

The first men to walk the very earliest beaches at Cape Krusenstern were the Denbigh Flint people. When they arrived, some five thousand years ago, most of the glaciers had melted, and sea level since has never risen enough to destroy their sites. The beaches where Denbigh camps are found near the northwestern tip of Cape Krusenstern now lie well inland — a mile and a half from the sea. . . .

Our first look at the craftsmanship of these meticulous flint-workers was at an extensive site at Cape Denbigh that we excavated between 1948 and 1952 . . . and in our subsequent years at Cape Krusenstern we were pleased to find that Denbigh people had been here too — on the now most inland ridges. In this windblown but mosquito-free location, they erected windbreaks and tents along the sea edge waiting for seals to swim past, and they left as evidence a litter of hearths with oval patches of charcoal, fired pebbles, and flint chips. . . .

Many of the broad, thin points found at these coastal sites, but not in the interior, offer as much proof as can be expected from stone tools alone that these people lived in spring or summer tents while pursuing seals and walruses with toggle harpoons essentially like those used by modern Eskimos.

J. Louis Giddings[1]

I remember that my father and grandfather were deeply moved by such places as Grand Canyon, Mesa Verde, Canyon de Chelly. And so was I when it came my turn as a park ranger among the Navajo people of the Southwest. That's why I feel at home here in Alaska, where traditional use by local people will continue in these new parklands. When the next beach ridge is formed here at Cape Krusenstern, I'd want some future regional director to stroll this shore and discover its meanings, as I have, with an Eskimo whose ancestors are buried in this ground.

John E. Cook

In many parts of the Eskimo domain the sea ice is constantly in motion, sometimes with imperceptible slowness, but always with a hugeness which betrays tremendous power. By contrast, the movement can be almost violently rapid. . . . Eskimos have amassed a large body of knowledge of the sea ice which permits them to move in comparative safety over it during their everyday activities. They are experts in ice lore, and we who know little of it can learn from them.

During the clear cold months of winter the best sign of open water is the heavy "steam fog," or *puguroak,* which forms due to contact of salt water with air that is over 14°C below the water temperature. . . . When the sky is clear, the only warning of ice breaking away between the hunter and the shore is usually the appearance of steam fog. At times of potential danger he watches carefully toward the shore again and again to assure that he is not caught on the far side of a widening crack. If the sun shines from behind the resultant steam fog, it might be difficult to detect the

"Whale Hunters Under Sail" by Kivetoruk Moses courtesy of the Anchorage Historical and Fine Arts Museum

crack, so the danger of being set adrift is greater. Steam fog can also be a guide for crossing a lead, since areas where it is not rising are indicators of solid ice. . . .

Clouds are another important factor in locating open water and navigating on the sea ice. . . . Clouds often create difficulties for the sea-ice hunter, [but] they can also be of service to him. When skies are overcast, a "sky map" is often present. The sky map is a reflection in the clouds of the color of the surface beneath it. . . .

For instance, during the winter sea ice reflects as dull white and the snow-covered land as a brilliant white. A traveler can trace the trend of the coastline far ahead of his position by reading the sky map. If he is out on the ice, he can tell from it which way he should go to reach the land. The most pronounced type of sky map, however, is the water sky [*Kissuk*], a dark streak in the clouds reflecting an open lead below.

Polar bears often catch seals by waiting for them at their breathing holes, small openings through the ice where seals come periodically for air. Seals are extremely cautious when they come to these holes, and the bear has evolved elaborate behavior patterns in order to succeed in hunting them. If polar bears could not catch seals at breathing holes, they probably could not survive through periods of midwinter when there is no open water.

The first thing a seal does when it comes to breathe is take a quick sniff of the air to detect danger. Thus, the bear must not station itself upwind of the hole. Eskimos say that they sit or lie on the ice at a right angle to the wind, and they may have to wait all day before a seal comes. . . .

If the breathing hole is in thin young ice, the bear simply waits until the seal comes and then smashes the surrounding ice with its front paws, simultaneously crushing the seal's skull. If the ice is thicker, the bear excavates the ice all around the hole, weakening it sufficiently so that it can carry out the same method of killing. It always fills the excavated area with snow so that when the seal swims up underneath, it cannot detect any change. Also, in thick ice the bear may dig a hole through the ice some distance from the breathing hole and wait there until it hears the sound of the seal's breathing. Then it slips silently through the hole and catches the seal by swimming up from beneath. . . .

Richard Nelson[2]

It was impossible to know when the seal would appear. In fifty winters of hunting at breathing holes, Sakiak had learned not to think too much of time. It might be fifteen minutes, perhaps an hour. Perhaps many hours. Sometimes the animal never returned. . . .

Young men said that breathing-hole hunting was too cold, that it involved too much waiting. The old men said only that people must eat. They had learned the art of enduring patience, as if they could merge their thoughts with the timeless physical world that surrounded them. Life, after all, was a game of waiting. One could not expect that the weather, ice, and animals

would do a man's bidding. If a man would live, he must persist, wait, endure.

Richard Nelson[3]

The men were still out hunting but there were no boats in view. I brought out crackers and made coffee for the women who were working nearby. Okukchuk was making a seal poke . . . . First she cut off the seal's head; then after skinning and scraping it, she turned the hide inside out and sewed all the openings closed except for a small hole at top. Inserting a small hollow bone into the hole, she blew up the seal poke to dry; then she rubbed ashes on the blown-up form. The hair acted as an insulator and the dried poke became an excellent airtight container.

An experienced Eskimo housewife, Okukchuk said: "Whale meat tastes much better in a seal poke than if I pack it in a barrel." I admired the ease with which she worked; she did everything smoothly, evidently enjoying her labor. It made me feel ashamed of the way I tackled unpleasant jobs; Okukchuk knew the art of doing necessary menial jobs with grace.

Claire Fejes[4]

That's Tuligak. He always hunt when he can. His wife's a good shooter too. He's *innupiak,* a real Eskimo.

an Eskimo elder

When the land was part of Siberia...

Seward Peninsula — western extremity of the American main — preserves the physical evidence and the ecological echoes of Beringia, the broad region that united East and West during the glacial epoch. Today's remnant, sometimes bizarre landscapes convey an unusually powerful sense of relationship between the present and the past. Here, as in a museum collection, can be traced the sequence of Ice Age geological events, environmental conditions, and biological and cultural evolution. Early man joined the procession that crossed the bridge, one species among many, sustained by his fellow migrants on the long marches from the Old World to the New. The dynamics continue — in the changing physical world and in the evolving life descended from the early colonists.

The land bridge emerged several times during the past million years when great ice sheets of the Pleistocene epoch spread out from the polar regions, locking up enormous quantities of water as ice and snow. World sea level dropped several hundred feet. This was enough to expose the shallow bottom of the Bering and Chukchi seas, creating between Siberia and Alaska a dry-land connection that lasted for thousands of years each time.

The lowlands of what is now the Seward Peninsula and the Yukon drainage were surrounded by fluctuating glaciers and seas. Shifting communities of plants and animals ebbed and flowed with alternating glacial and warmer periods. Spruce trees retreated during colder times to be replaced by dwarf forests, tundra, and arctic steppe. During landbridge intervals, the arctic steppe, similar to the sage-and-grass plains of Idaho, attracted from Siberia a startling array of wildlife — elephants, lions, camels, antelopes, and many others, including today's surviving species such as moose, bear, wolf, and lynx. Men, too, were caught in the movement. All of these species, cut off from temperate zones by walls of ice, found refuge in the continental expanse of the arctic steppelands of Siberia and Alaska.

By the time the last ice advance began to melt and retreat, many waves of human pioneers had followed the track of the northern lights to the New World. Some of these ancestors of the Indians stayed in Alaska; others slipped between the shifting icefields to colonize all of North and South America. The ancestors of the Eskimos, whose descendents still live on the Seward Peninsula, may have arrived before the last submergence of the land bridge some 11,000 years ago. Or they may have come by sea as recently as 5,000 years ago. The rising seas that closed the land bridge did not totally isolate Asia from America, as ancient trade patterns attest. But after that event, the migrants evolved their cultures in a distinctively American way.

Before, during, and after the migrations across the land bridge, volcanism added new landforms to the Seward Peninsula. The Imuruk lava flows are notable for their extent and variety in the arctic environment and because they display unique effects of eruptive venting through permafrost. Another type of volcanics produced explosion craters called "maars," now lakes of crystal waters rimmed by ash, cinders, and scoria. These were formed when rising magma contacted moisture in the permafrost. The intense heat of the molten rock resulted in violent steam explosions that ripped great holes in the surface, often miles in diameter.

Sediments in these lakes, and in others caused by lava damming, provide valuable records of pollen rain that tell much of former vegetation and climate in this part of Beringia. More exciting is the Pompeii effect of the maar explosions. Their ashfalls covered large areas. The buried vegetation and other life forms quickly froze and remain perfectly preserved to this day. Thus, each ashfall holds intact a sampling of life at the moment of eruption.

Undulating tundra and scattered lakes occupy most of the preserve, which is bounded on the south by low mountains and on the north by the estuaries and barrier islands of the Chukchi Sea. No striking physical features interrupt the gentle slope of the plain toward

the sea. But nowhere is there a better transect of arctic tundra types nor a more representative segment of arctic shoreline.

This varied environment hosts great gatherings of migratory birds and marine animals. The Seward Peninsula lies at the crossroads of the Asiatic and North American flyway — continuing to serve as a steppingstone if not a bridge. Birds migrate here from all seven continents. A total of 170 species visit the area for staging and breeding, the greater number of them shorebirds. The rich coastal waters attract 15 species of sea mammals, including 8 species of whales.

Thus, this place remains a choice area for hunters and gatherers. The scattered communities of Eskimos bordering the area continue to subsist on its plants and wildlife and to capture the beluga whales that concentrate in the shallow waters sheltered by Cape Espenberg. Herds of reindeer — domesticated caribou imported from the Old World during a time of starvation — graze in those sections of the preserve historically used for this purpose.

The area within the preserve escaped most of the gold rush impacts that convulsed the Nome environs to the south. These lake and tundra barrens remain remote, seldom visited by the outside world. The preserve's subtle beauties are punctuated in only a few places, as at the scenic enclave of Serpentine Hot Springs, where crowning spires of rock recall an ancient geologic intrusion.

But scenery is not the compelling attraction here; rather, it is the story of the Bering Land Bridge, the saga of plants and animals and men finding refuge from the ice. Buried in the ashflows and sediments, hidden in the deposits of limestone caves, the fossils and artifacts of landbridge history have created a modern bridge of science between the two nations sharing the Bering Strait. ■

Eighteen years ago, stormbound at Wales village, I studied the mist smoking over a turbulent Bering Strait and wondered who, on this violent day, might be shouldering the wind on the Asian shore to share my search for traces of the past. Near me rose a peaty mound, the midden left by generation upon generation of Eskimos dwelling at the western tip of North America; behind me rose Cape Mountain, scarred by ancient glaciers, carved by ancient waves. Perhaps someone was at that moment sheltering his Cyrillic notes from the mist as he huddled on a terrace on East Cape, at the eastern tip of Siberia — or in an Eskimo burial ground at Uelen, Siberia's easternmost village.

That search — and the findings of my colleague on the other shore — have continued to fascinate me in the years since, and to draw substantially on my professional attention. For Bering Strait is the dramatic focal point of one of the world's great crossroads. The Strait itself is the one narrow avenue of sea communication between the North Pacific and the Arctic and North Atlantic Oceans, and, of course, it is the point where Asia lies only one day's umiak journey from North America. More significantly, it lies at the center of what has been, on several occasions in the past, the sole avenue for dryland migrations between the Old and New Worlds — and thus at the center of what was, during these occasions, the barrier partitioning North Pacific and North Atlantic marine biotas. For these reasons, the history of Beringia . . . has long excited the interest of geologists, biogeographers, [and] anthropologists. . . .

David M. Hopkins[1]

We approached the strait which separates the two great continents of Asia and America, on one of those beautiful still nights, well known to all who have visited the arctic regions, when the sky is without a cloud, and when the midnight sun, scarcely his own diameter below the horizon, tinges with a bright hue all the northern circle. Our ship, propelled by an increasing breeze, glided rapidly along a smooth sea, startling from her path flocks of lummes and dovekies, and other aquatic birds, whose flight could, from the stillness of the scene, be traced by the ear to a considerable distance. . . .

We closed with the American shore, a few miles to the northward of Cape Prince of Wales, and found the coast low, with a ridge of sand extending along it, on which we noticed several Esquimaux habitations. Steering along this shore to the northward, in ten and eight fathoms water, a little before noon we were within four and a half miles of Schismareff Inlet. . . .

We noticed upon [an island] a considerable village of yourts [skin tents], the largest of any that had as yet been seen. The natives appear to prefer having their dwellings upon this sandy foundation to the main land, probably on account of the latter being swampy, which is the case every where in the vicinity of this inlet and Kotzebue Sound. Several of them, taking advantage of the calm, came off in badairs. . . . [They] were noisy and energetic, but goodnatured; laughed much, and humorously apprized us when we were making a good bargain.

Capt. Frederick Beechey, 1831

During at least the last two episodes of continental glaciation, the only extensive area in northern North America that was not inundated by glacial ice and is not now under water was the great lowland lying between the Alaska and Brooks Ranges, and east into the Yukon Territory. There is abundant evidence that this area supported a complex and varied flora and fauna during the periods of time when most of the rest of northern North America was beneath ice.

The Bering Land Bridge periodically connected this part of Alaska with similarly unglaciated parts of Siberia, coincident with periods of continental glaciation. Biogeographically, then, interior and western Alaska has been a part of Asia, rather than North America, during probably the majority of the past million years. The

most recent sundering of this connection took place only 10-13,000 years ago. The peripheral areas on either side of Bering Strait which escaped inundation may be thought of as remnants of the great landscape known as Beringia, but the sea's encroachment brought a marked change in climate to the region, and the biota has changed accordingly.

During glacial periods, the climate of Beringia was undoubtedly colder than at present on an annual basis. Because the climate was essentially continental, however, bitterly cold winters were probably offset by summers warmer and drier than today. Many students of Beringia, on the basis of paleontological and other evidence, have concluded that this ancient environment was largely characterized by a semi-arid grassland called the arctic steppe or steppe-tundra.

It has long been known that this landscape supported a much greater variety of large and small mammals than is presently found in the region. Some species, such as the woolly mammoth and long-horned bison, became extinct at about the time of the final submergence of the land bridge. Other species, such as the saiga antelope, continue to exist elsewhere, but no longer occur in the Beringian region. In view of the variety of the mammalian fauna that the region was able to support, it has been hypothesized that the ancient environment was qualitatively different from the present environment, or, indeed, any environment presently existing in the far north. Some workers believe that ice-age Beringia supported a biome that has no present counterpart on the face of the earth. There are today many unusual vegetational communities in the Beringian area — these may be relicts of a vanished or nearly vanished biome and so are of great interest to biogeographers.

adapted from Steve Young[2]

I am impressed that late-glacial remains of the saiga, a steppe antelope restricted to central Asia today, have been found in Interior and Arctic Alaska for that

Mammoth tusks from Fredrick W. Beechey, *Narrative of a Voyage to the Pacific and Bering Strait,* vol. 2, Da Cape Press, New York, 1968, plate 2 would seem to demand landscapes that offer the firm footing this small-hooved animal requires — conditions entirely at odds with what exists today. Yet steppe-like landscapes do not require the wholesale invention of a biome but merely dramatic changes in the ranges and relative importance of plant groups already in existence.

David Murray[3]

One of the most intriguing aspects of the area is that the general features of the terrain are today essentially the same as they were when the land was part of Siberia, because this land was never glaciated except for small areas in the mountains. And the visitor who stumbles, as I did, on a mammoth skull rolling in the surf of a Bering Strait beach can easily imagine early hunting parties stealthily pursuing these huge shaggy beasts across the rolling hills or near one of the many lowland lakes.

T. Stell Newman[4]

The Bering Strait area is still commonly visualized as a narrow path or trail over which people hustled, in one direction, on their way to take up positions in which they would presently be discovered. The view presented here is that, in fact, the Bering Land Bridge was an enormous continental area extending nearly 1,500 km from its southern extremity, now the eastern Aleutians, to its northern margin in the Arctic Ocean. It was an area that could accommodate many permanent residents, human and animal, and it endured for a longer time than that documented for the entire period of human occupancy in America.

William Laughlin[5]

In 1975 joint Soviet-American archeological excavations took place at Lake Baikal in Siberia.

People of the early Bronze Age buried their dead on the edge of a high prominence [near here]. Excavations . . .yielded interesting and important material — burials with stone and bone artifacts.

We were most anxious to see whether the skeletons resembled American Indians, Eskimos or Aleuts. For this reason, Professor William Laughlin waited impatiently for the soil to be cleared away from the skeletons of the Stone and Bronze Age people. When the remains were finally uncovered, he picked up a skull and exclaimed: "No, it's not an Eskimo! It's an Indian!"

Based upon the evidence at hand, we arrived at the same conclusion that had been voiced tentatively by our predecessor, Ales Hrdlicka, many years ago: the most ancient inhabitants of the Lake Baikal area were genetically closer to American Indians than to Eskimos and Aleuts.

The majority of Soviet scientists are of the opinion that the first men appeared on the American continent about 27,000 to 25,000 years ago. According to Professor Laughlin — and I am of the same opinion — the first group to arrive in the New World was small, consisting only of about 500 people. From this small group, the population grew, and by the time Christopher Columbus landed in 1492, it had reached three million.

Current research by scientists of many nationalities proves that an ancient land bridge did exist. Few dispute the assertion that the route "the first Americans" followed into the New World lay precisely on the land bridge. As hunters directly dependent on animals that supplied them with everything they needed — food, clothing, fuel — the Paleo-Asians moved farther and farther into the interior of the unexplored regions following the animals that had migrated in search of better feeding grounds.

Traces of Paleolithic hunters' campfires and the remains of their activities in the form of stone arrowheads, knives, scrapers and other tools, are found over a vast area, from the Gobi Desert to the plateau

AFTERWORD

prairies of America. They mark the route of groups who migrated from central Asia to America over the millennia.

A.P. Okladnikov[6]

After spending more than an hour threading our way through fields of broken lava, we finally reached the low crest of the old cinder cone. Here we found [ancient] cairns of all sorts of shapes and sizes constructed of stacked slabs of flat lava. Some cairns were only a yard high, but others were well over ten feet in height. All were covered with a dense covering of mosses and lichens. Several guesses have been made about why they were built, ranging from the usual "religious structure" — the most ready explanation for something we don't understand — through navigational aids for use on the featureless winter landscape, to structures used for channeling caribou herds into areas where they could be more readily killed. I don't know what they are, and neither does anyone else. But this lack of understanding doesn't detract from their significance; in fact, their mystery may enhance their value.

In the springtime the darkness of winter changes to almost perpetual sunlight; the snow begins to melt and the lakes and streams to thaw. Yet, long before the sea ice and the snowbanks on the land are gone, the entire area comes vibrantly alive. Birds from all over the world begin to arrive in vast numbers: ducks, geese, brant, sandhill cranes, and swans wing in to spend the summer in the wet lowland tundra, and shorebirds come to both the coast and the upland tundra. The upland tundra also is the summer home for many species of songbirds.... a number of species of birds come to the preserve from the Old World: Asia, Europe, and even Africa. This is one of the few places in the nation where these Old World species may be routinely seen.

T. Stell Newman[7]

It is fitting that this journey should end on a remnant of the Bering Land Bridge. The land and life forms of this place — both active and of the past — speak eloquently of Nature's mighty rhythms. Deaths and vanishings have occurred here many times. And, as often, renewals. Imprinted in the rocks and in the living plants and animals are codes and messages from ages past. Both carriers and codes have been shaped and reshaped by the changing world. Yet, the tern that flies so far to get here carries inside itself the ancient discovery first registered in the brain of its ancestor.

There will be other times. New ice sheets, new lands emerging. Creatures and plants made for today's conditions will change their fur and feathers, their leaves and roots, to meet whatever comes. Migrants through these seas will visit other scenes when the land bridge rises again.

So the great cycles roll on. And we are privileged to have the intellectual gifts that let us decipher these codes and understand a few of these mysteries. We can stand on this bridge and reconstruct the pageant. We can watch our own ancestors, mingled with the others, coming to this always New World.

In this strange landscape, by happenstance of our time here, now bordered by barren mountains and cold seas, we can reach a little way into the depths that surround our existence. We can touch for a moment the current of which we are a part.

In the Alaska national parklands we can feel that current still moving.

from Louis J. Giddings, *Ancient Men of the Arctic*, Alfred A. Knopf, New York, 1977

LITERATURE CREDITS & NOTES

Many publishers and individuals permitted the use of selections presented in this book. Copyrighted materials and selected major references are credited below. In addition, many personal and public-domain selections are credited by author or title in the text.

INTRODUCTION

[1]With permission from *Natural History,* May, 1981, copyright The American Museum of Natural History, 1981, from "The Tourist as Pilgrim," by Colin Turnbull, George Washington University.

GLACIER BAY NATIONAL PARK & PRESERVE

[1]John Muir, *Travels in Alaska,* Houghton Mifflin Co., 1915, pp. 146, 148-149. [2]*Harriman Alaska Expedition, 1899,* Vol. I, Narrative of the Voyage, Doubleday, New York, 1901. [3]Dave Bohn, *Glacier Bay: The Land and the Silence,* orig. published by the Sierra Club, San Francisco, 1967, reprinted by Alaska Natural History Association, 1977, p. 4. By permission of author. [4]William O. Field, "Glacier Recession in Muir Inlet," *The Geographical Review,* American Geographical Society, New York, July 1947, p. 369. By permission of publisher. [5]William S. Cooper, *Ecology,* Vol. IV, No. 3, 1923 and Vol. XX, No. 2, 1929. [6]With permission from American Geographical Society, from Reid's Glacier Bay field journal for 1892. [7]Charles Jurasz, "Alaska Whales and Whaling," ALASKA GEOGRAPHIC, Vol. 5, No. 4, copyright 1978, The Alaska Geographic Society, Box 4-EEE, Anchorage, Alaska 99509. [8]Charles Jurasz, "Among 30-Ton Whales: Good Luck by Mistake," *Defenders of Wildlife,* 54, April 1978, pp. 83-84. [9]Greg Streveler, "Distribution, Population Ecology, and Impact Susceptibility of the Harbor Seal in Glacier Bay, Alaska," National Park Service report, Juneau, 1979. [10]Reprinted by permission of the Smithsonian Institution Press, from *Smithsonian Contributions to Anthropology,* Vol. 7; "Under Mount Saint Elias; The History and Culture of the Yakutat Tlingit," by Frederica DeLaguna, Smithsonian Institution, Washington, D.C., 1972. [11]Dave Bohn, *Glacier Bay: The Land and the Silence,* p. 35. [12]Vi Swanson Kreutzer, "Trapped in an Eighty-Foot Tidal Wave," *ALASKA* Magazine, Anchorage, Sept. 1980, p. 19. By permission of author and publisher.

SITKA NATIONAL HISTORICAL PARK

[1]Polly Miller, *Lost Heritage of Alaska,* Bonanza Books, New York, 1967, a valuable source of original accounts. [2]Hubert Howe Bancroft, *The History of Alaska,* A.L. Bancroft & Co., San Francisco, 1886. [3]From *Early Visitors to Southeastern Alaska — Nine Accounts,* edited by R.N. DeArmond, copyright 1978; Alaska Northwest Publishing Company, Box 4-EEE, Anchorage, Alaska 99509, p. 91. By permission of publisher. [4]Richard Dauenhauer, from forthcoming "Occasional Papers of the Center for Cross Cultural Studies," University of Alaska, Fairbanks, 1982. By permission of author. [5]From

"Because We Cherish You," Sealaska Elders Speak to the Future, transcribed, translated and edited by Nora Dauenhauer and Richard Dauenhauer, Sealaska Heritage Foundation Press, Juneau, Alaska, 1981. By permission of publisher.

KLONDIKE GOLD RUSH NATIONAL HISTORICAL PARK

[1]Pierre Berton, *The Klondike Fever,* copyright 1958 by Alfred A. Knopf, Inc., pp. 150-151. By permission of publisher. [2]Robert Spude, *Chilkoot Trail,* copyright 1980 by Anthropology and Historic Preservation, Cooperative Park Studies Unit, University of Alaska, Fairbanks. All Chilkoot Pass selections from Spude.

KATMAI NATIONAL PARK & PRESERVE

[1]Dave Bohn, *Rambles Through an Alaskan Wild: Katmai and the Valley of the Smokes,* Capra Press, 1979, p. 149. By permission of the author. [2]*Ibid.,* p. 86. [3]G.H. Curtis, "Importance of Novarupta During the Eruption of Mt. Katmai, Alaska, in 1912," Bull. Geol. Soc. of America, Vol. 66, 1955. [4]Robert F. Griggs, *The Valley of Ten Thousand Smokes,* The National Geographic Society, Washington, D.C., 1922, p. 191. By permission of publisher. [5]*Ibid.,* p. 201. [6]*Ibid.,* p. 217. [7]By permission of the Smithsonian Misc. Col., Vol. 138, No. 5, *A Biological Survey of Katmai National Monument,* by V.H. Cahalane, Smithsonian Institution, Washington, D.C., 1959. [8]Reprinted by permission from *National Parks Magazine,* March, 1978, copyright by National Parks and Conservation Association, p. 37. [9]Dave Bohn, *op. cit.,* pp. 112-113. [10]From the Baked Mountain Cabin Log, on file at Katmai National Park and Preserve.

ANIAKCHAK NATIONAL MONUMENT & PRESERVE

[1]Bernard Hubbard, "A World Inside a Mountain," *National Geographic Magazine,* The National Geographic Society, Washington, D.C., copyright 1931.

KENAI FJORDS NATIONAL PARK

[1]John Madson, "Kenai Fjords: National Park in Waiting," reprinted from AUDUBON, the magazine of the National Audubon Society, copyright 1978, pp. 56, 58.

LAKE CLARK NATIONAL PARK & PRESERVE

[1]Quoted in John Kauffmann, "Lake Clark, The Essence of Alaska: Tundra, Glaciers, Mountains," in *Exploring America's Backcountry,* National Geographic Society, Washington, D.C., 1979, p. 201. By permission of publisher. [2]*Ibid.,* p. 179. [3]*Ibid.* [4]Courtesy of Richard Proenneke, framed on his cabin wall. [5]From *One Man's Wilderness,* by Richard Proenneke, pp. 3, 7, 14, 64-66, 73. Copyright 1977, Alaska Northwest Publishing Company, Box 4-EEE, Anchorage, Alaska 99509.

WRANGELL-SAINT ELIAS NATIONAL PARK & PRESERVE

[1]Prepared by members of U.S. Geological Survey, *Landscapes of Alaska, Their Geologic Evolution,* University of California Press, Berkeley, copyright 1958 by the Regents of the University of California, pp. 20-21. By permission of publisher. [2]Melody Webb Grauman, *Big Business in Alaska: The Kennecott Mines, 1898-1938,* National Park Service, 1977. [3]The Wrangell Mountain Project, University of California, Santa Cruz, in Public Testimony at San Francisco, May 1973. [4]From "Ordeal in the North," by Ned Gillette, reprinted by permission of SKI Magazine, December, 1975. [5]Permission granted for quote from *One Long Summer Day in Alaska* by Donald C. Defenderfer and Robert B. Walkinshaw, Publication no. 8, Environmental Field Program, University of California, Santa Cruz, 1981, pp. 33, 49.

INTERIOR PARKLANDS

[1]Prepared by members of U.S. Geological Survey, *Landscapes of Alaska, Their Geologic Evolution,* University of California Press, Berkeley, copyright 1958 by the Regents of the University of California.

YUKON-CHARLEY RIVERS NATIONAL PRESERVE

[1]John McPhee, *Coming into the Country,* copyright 1976, 1977 by John McPhee. This material first appeared in *The New Yorker.* Reprinted by permission of the publisher, Farrar, Straus and Giroux, Inc., p. 190. [2]Melody Webb Grauman, *Yukon Frontiers,* Anthropology and Historic Preservation, Cooperative Park Studies Unit, University of Alaska, Fairbanks, 1977. [3]Quoted from John Haines, "Three Days," in *Minus 31 and the Wind Blowing,* Alaska Pacific University Press, 1980, pp. 22-23. [4]McPhee, *op. cit.,* p. 278. [5]From *Two in the Far North,* by Margaret E. Murie, p. 10. Copyright 1978, Alaska Northwest Publishing Company, Box 4-EEE, Anchorage, Alaska 99509. [6]From the unpublished manuscript "Another Man's Life," memoirs of C.A. Bryant, courtesy of Alaska Historical Library, Juneau. [7]Steve Young, *The Environment of the Yukon-Charley Rivers Area, Alaska,* Center for Northern Studies, Wolcott, Vermont, 1976. [8]Carol Allison, personal communication with author, 1978. [9]John Seiberling, quoted in *Alaska: Wilderness Frontier* by Boyd Norton, Reader's Digest Press, New York, 1977. [10]Gary Holthaus, "Some Years Winter," in *Unexpected Manna,* Copper Canyon Press, 1978.

DENALI NATIONAL PARK & PRESERVE

[1]Charles Sheldon, *The Wilderness of Denali,* copyright 1930 by Charles Scribner's Sons; copyright renewed 1958 by Louisa Sheldon. Reprinted with permission of Charles Scribner's Sons. [2]Harry Karstens, describing the first climb to the summit in a letter to Charles Sheldon, Archives of the University of Alaska, Fairbanks. Slightly edited for punctuation. [3]From "Quest" with permission of Bruce Duncan. [4]Grant Pearson, *The Seventy Mile Kid,* Signal Press, copyright 1957. [5]Ginny Hill Wood and Celia Hunter, "The Tundra Telegram," 1960. [6]Adolph Murie, *A Naturalist in Alaska,* copyright 1961 by

Devin Adair Co., Old Greenwich, Ct. 06870, p. 8. By permission of publisher. [7]Adolph Murie, *Mammals of Mt. McKinley National Park, Alaska,* Alaska Natural History Association, Anchorage, 1962, p. 1. [8]Adolph Murie, *A Naturalist in Alaska,* pp. 278-280, 259-260, 242-243. [9]Olaus Murie, *Journeys to the Far North,* The Wilderness Society and Crown Publishers, 1973, pp. 121, 46. [10]Adolph Murie, *A Naturalist in Alaska,* pp. 293-296, 30-31.

GATES OF THE ARCTIC NATIONAL PARK & PRESERVE

[1]Robert Marshall, *Alaska Wilderness — Exploring the Central Brooks Range,* University of California Press, Berkeley, copyright 1956, 1970 by the Regents of the University of California, pp. 12, 103-104. By permission of publisher. [2]Russell Train, former chairman, Council on Environmental Quality, testifying in favor of Alaska Lands Act, 1978. [3]Quoted in Kenneth Brower, *Earth and the Great Weather,* Friends of the Earth, San Francisco, 1971, p. 141. By permission of publisher. [4]Joe McGinness, *Going to Extremes,* Alfred A. Knopf, New York, copyright 1980 by Joe McGinness, reprinted by arrangement with The New American Library, Inc., New York, N.Y., pp. 255, 266. [5]From *Two in the Far North,* by Margaret Murie, p. 325. Copyright 1978, Alaska Northwest Publishing Company, Box 4-EEE, Anchorage, Alaska 99509. [6]Lois Crisler, *Arctic Wild,* Harper & Row, New York, 1958, p. 136. [7]Billie Wright, *Four Seasons North,* Harper & Row, New York, 1973, pp. 57, 87. [8]Kenneth Brower, *op. cit.,* p. 53. [9]Quoted by permission of the Bancroft Library. [10]Robert Marshall, "The Problem of the Wilderness," *Scientific Monthly,* Vol. 30, No. 2, 1930. [11]Boyd Norton, *Alaska: Wilderness Frontier,* Reader's Digest Press, New York, 1977, p. 37. By permission of author. [12]Reprinted by permission of *National Parks Magazine,* Jan.-Mar. 1958, copyright 1958 by National Parks and Conservation Association. [13]Kenneth Brower, *op. cit.,* p. 72.

NOATAK NATIONAL PRESERVE

[1]Steve Young, *The Environment of the Noatak River Basin, Alaska,* The Center for Northern Studies, Wolcott, Vermont, 1974. [2]*Ibid.*

KOBUK VALLEY NATIONAL PARK

[1]Quoted in Douglas Anderson, *et al., Kuuvangmiit Subsistence: Traditional Eskimo Life in the Latter Twentieth Century,* National Park Service, Washington, D.C., 1977. [2]J. Louis Giddings, *Ancient Men of the Arctic,* copyright 1967 by Ruth W. Giddings, Executrix of the Estate of J. Louis Giddings. Reprinted by permission of Alfred A. Knopf, Inc., pp. 305-6, 316, 317, 319-20, 344-45. [3]*Ibid.,* p. 346. [4]*Ibid.,* pp. 349-51, 352, 354. [5]By Ole Wik from "Kotzebue Basin," ALASKA GEOGRAPHIC, Vol. 8, No. 3, pp. 42-43. Copyright 1981, The Alaska Geographic Society, Box 4-EEE, Anchorage, Alaska 99509. [6]Joseph Meeker, "Alaska's Indigenous Lifestyle," in *Minus 31 and the Wind Blowing,* Alaska Pacific University Press, 1980, pp. 94-95. By permission of publisher.

CAPE KRUSENSTERN NATIONAL MONUMENT

[1]J. Louis Giddings, *Ancient Men of the Arctic,* (see above permission), pp. 223-24, 64, 123, 176-77, 230-31, 244-45, 246. [2]Richard Nelson, *Hunters of the Northern Ice,* University of Chicago Press, copyright 1969, University of Chicago, pp. 9-10, 265-266, 268-269, 187-188. By permission of author and publisher. [3]Richard Nelson, *Shadow of the Hunter,* University of Chicago Press, copyright 1980, University of Chicago, pp. 15, 16. By permission of author and publisher. [4]Claire Fejes, *People of the Noatak,* Alfred A. Knopf, 1974, p. 33. By permission of author.

BERING LAND BRIDGE NATIONAL PRESERVE

[1]David M. Hopkins, ed., *The Bering Land Bridge,* Stanford University Press, Stanford, 1967, p. vii. [2]Steve Young, *et al., Proposed Geological and Ecological Natural Landmarks in Interior and Western Alaska,* Center for Northern Studies, Wolcott, Vt., 1982. [3]David Murray, "The Role of Arctic Refugia in the Evolution of the Arctic Vascular Flora — A Beringian Perspective," Institute of Arctic Biology and the Museum, University of Alaska, Fairbanks, 1981. [4]T. Stell Newman, "Bering Land Bridge: Arctic Causeway to the New World," in *Wilderness Parklands in Alaska,* National Parks and Conservation Association, Washington, D.C., 1978, p. 43. [5]"Human Migration and Permanent Occupation in the Bering Sea Area," in David M. Hopkins, ed., *The Bering Land Bridge,* p. 410. [6]A. P. Okladnikov, "The Ancient Bridge," *Alaska Journal,* Vol. 9, No. 4, Autumn 1979, p. 45. [7]T. Stell Newman, *op. cit.,* pp. 46, 47.

Back Cover: Debbie Martinez, testimony in favor of the Alaska Lands Act of 1980.

John E. Cook, Regional Director for the National Park Service in Alaska, assisted the creators of this book variously with time, tools, and, most important, trust. When the issue was in doubt, he spurred us on. He wanted a book that would requite the interest of those who know and want to know the values of these Alaska national parklands.

The author bows to his title-page colleagues, who made this book possible through endurance, encouragement and *hard* work.

John Kauffmann was the author's guru. He provided the wise counsel of a seasoned Alaskan adventurer and bookman.

Judy Brogan edited text and smoothed syntax with skill and good humor.

Robert Belous, Ray Bane, and Greg Streveler provided technical counsel.

Tamara Glauner typed the shifting piles of manuscript, accurately.

The Board of Directors of the Alaska Natural History Association had faith and took the risk. Other cooperating associations around the country provided wherewithal to complete the project.

Finally, innumerable people — some on park staffs, some in the interested public — gave materials and critique to help us.

PHOTOGRAPHY CREDITS

Tom Bean - cover, 12, 13, 17, 20, 84-85, 99; David Buchanan - 80; Brad Carlquist - 64; David L. Cohen - 29; Sue Eddlestein - 26; Meg Jensen - 9; John Johnson - 84 (*bear*), 99; Penny Knuckles - 42; Rick McIntyre - 84 (*caribou*); Elizabeth Mills - 37, 99 (*2*); John Morris - 53 (*cliff nests*); National Park Service - 45, 51, 59, 61, 63, 96, 102, 107, 115; B. E. Norton - 45, 49, 52, 55, 67, 71, 72, 121; Danny On - 53 (*oyster catcher*), 84 (*fox*), 99; Tommy Ongtovguk - 108-109, 113; Rollie Ostermick - 41, 53 (*puffin*), 69, 89, 110; Catherine Rezabeck - 93; Helen Rhodes - 84 (*ground squirrel*); Jim Shives - 99 (*4*); Walter Smalling - 22; Mike Tollefson - 56; Tom Walker - 53 (*kittiwakes*); Dick Wood - 74, 79, 101.

Printed by Paragon Press, Inc., Salt Lake City, Utah